Swan Lake 2

Don Sweetenham

REFLECTIONS

ON

SWAN LAKE – 2

BY

D.J. "Don" SWEETENHAM

Humming birds, insects, ducks, swans, geese and

numerous

other creatures feature in these stories

of their activities in, on and around the lake.

Having the time and the place to observe Nature in

all her Glory, is one of the few benefits of being retired.

Being able to share these stories with you is a rare honor

for me.

DEDICATION and THANKS

This book is dedicated to the members of The Heritage Writers Group, my wife, Millie and Mickie and Seth Jackson of The Henry County Times. Sincere thanks to Sharon Davidson and PJ Renfroe, for their encouragement and their technical expertise without which this endeavor would never have been realized. Special thanks go to those readers who have commented on my columns in The Henry County Times and, of course, to my two Best Buddies, Sam and Dee and all the wild life in, on and around Swan Lake. Thanks for your support and Best Wishes to y'all!

Don.

Most of the stories in this book, written by D.J. Sweetenham, were originally published in The Henry County Times. However, these stories are the property of the author and none may be copied in any media without written permission of

D.J. Sweetenham.

E&OE

CONTENTS

SOLO ARRIVES

One morning, as we (that is Sam, Dee and I) were getting ready to go visit with our friend Doc, I heard a cheery "Hey, Don" and looked up to see my neighbor, Pam, the Duck Lady, walking one of her dogs. I put the Kids in the car so they wouldn't cause a fuss with the other dog and then joined Pam for a few moments. She asked me if I had noticed a stray white Pekin duck at our early morning feeding time. I told her that I had noticed something unusual way out on the outskirts of the feeding frenzy that morning but as it was just before dawn, the light was too dim for me to identify it. Whatever it was, it was too shy to come in close enough to get any food and it didn't hang around very long afterwards. She told me that it was not one of her Pekins but a stray which had suddenly appeared. She thought it was probably released on the lake by someone who had been given the duckling at Easter and it had just become too much trouble to look after when it became an adult. She said she had been able to give it some food and hoped that it would soon get accustomed to mixing in with the other wild birds.

The next morning I looked out for the lone Pekin and again found her on the far edge of the pack. This time I made a real effort to throw food her way and she managed to snatch a few pieces without coming in closer. She must have enjoyed the few morsels which she managed to gobble up because after that, she found enough courage to barge her way through the crowd of smaller ducks, and even geese, to get her fair share.

It took no more than a couple of days until Solo, as Pam named her, overcame her fears and joined in the morning mealtime melee and she now holds her own, pushing and shoving her way through the crowd to get

her breakfast. She has a loud, distinctive "quaaark",

which she doesn't hesitate to use if I am a little late in the

morning, by her reckoning. She has also taken up a

leadership role with about a dozen or so female Mallards

who follow behind her when she paddles away. It looks

a bit like the Lake Ladies Club. So that's what LLC

stands for. I've always wondered!

About a week ago, when the weather was

unseasonably warm, the Kids and I were enjoying our

afternoon picnic with no ducks or geese near the boat to

kick up a fuss. Before we had boarded the boat, I had

taken a dipper full of food along to the feed box on the

dock for Lucy the white goose. I could hear her

grumbling and mumbling to herself, probably over the

fact that the feeder was empty. She greeted me noisily

when she saw that I brought food and tucked into it like

an eating machine as soon as it hit the floor of the feeder. It's so nice to be appreciated, even if her greeting is a deafening cross between a bellow and a scream. I know it is just a goose term of affection and I love her for it.

So I was sitting in the Captain's chair enjoying my ripe banana snack while the Kids demolished their two bowls of Kibbles. The sun was shining, there was no wind and everything was relatively quiet on board. Just the muted sound of Kibbles being munched and Lucy at the other end of the sea wall, tapping away at the food in the feeder box. I must have been nodding off a little, in the warm sunshine. It's something us old f........ellows do, you know. Suddenly there was a loud "Rat-a-tat-tat" on the side of the boat, immediately behind me. I jumped up, dropping the remains of my banana on the deck, swung around and stumbled and tripped over the two Kids who were loudly protecting the boat from Big Daddy, the male swan, who had sneaked up on us from behind.

"What the heck was that?" I shouted, or words to that effect, before I was fully aware of what was going on. Big Daddy continued to rap on the aluminum boat side until I told him to "Shut up" and gave him a handful of the kids' Kibbles. Then we had a little heart-to-heart talk about his behavior at feeding time in the morning and I made him promise to eat the food which I throw to him and to leave the others to eat theirs before he charges off to aggravate the Canadas.

I don't know if our little talk did any good but since then things have been a lot more civilized at breakfast. I'd like to think that I got through to him but that may just be "Wishful thinking!"

LUCY LOST HER MOJO

For a while there, Lucy was Queen of the Lake, after she lost her temper with Big Daddy and gave him the beating which he richly deserved. It was a real treat for all the spectator ducks and geese to see Big Daddy, the male swan, flapping and struggling against the very angry and determined female white goose hanging onto his tail feathers. Everyone thought that the big bully's days as Master of the Lake had expired. With Lucy's gentle, nurturing personality, it was hoped that peace would reign over the lake once more, as it did before the Swans arrived. And so it did, for a month or so. But then Big Daddy started to regain his confidence. He initially practiced his antagonistic behavior on the Canada geese who are much too gentle to try and fight back and he just wasn't fast enough to latch onto many ducks. He still couldn't catch Dodger, the gray goose and leader of the Canadas. No matter how hard he tried, Dodger still made a fool of him.

By now, of course, Lucy had long forgotten the discomfort and humiliation she had previously suffered at the beak of Big Daddy. One morning, when she was quietly pecking away at the food which I had placed in her feeder box, Big Daddy quietly paddled around the corner of the dock and pounced on her before she could even get her head out of the box. It didn't last long. Lucy was smart enough to dive quickly and Big Daddy had to let go. She surfaced underneath the dock which was too close to the water for Big Daddy to follow her. Frustrated, he patrolled around the perimeter of the dock for a few minutes before moving away to stand tall in the water and flap his wings in a victory display. It was obvious to all of us watching, that poor Lucy was again going to be the number one recipient of Big Daddy's attention. While he was preening himself, forlorn and shocked, she paddled away from the dock, back to her roosting site in the Northern end of the Lake. We all felt so sorry for her but there was not much that any of us could have done to help her. However, Lucy and I have worked out a new feeding routine which might be an improvement.

In the morning when all the gang gathers, I first put half a scoop in the feeder box. This gives Lucy a quick snack before Big Daddy shows up to drive her away. She doesn't give him time to catch her before she heads North and by the time he gets back to the feeder box, it's empty. He's slowly beginning to realize that he has to get his breakfast with the rest of the birds, if he wants anything to eat. In the afternoons the Kids and I go down to the boat for our picnic and I take a scoop of duck food with us. As soon as I see that Lucy is waiting by the feeder box, I give her the rest of her 'breakfast'. We then make our way back to the boat, watching out for Big Daddy all the way.

Anyway, we'll just have to wait and see how things progress between Lucy and the Big Bully. I can sympathize with her as I had similar experiences with bullies at two of the schools which I attended as a boy in England. I was only seven years old when the family moved to a country area where all the kids had a different accent from me. This was their excuse for picking on me and soon I was getting beaten up, almost on a daily basis. I made sure that, when I changed schools, no-one would pick on me again. I had learned a few things from those beatings and I broke the nose of the first boy to speak to me at the new school. All bullies are cowards, anyway, and I have no time for any of them.

A GEORGIA GRAY DRIZZLY DAY

It's just one of those days. A steady, fine rain is falling from a gloomy, overcast sky. There's no sign of any wildlife but on the far side of the Lake, someone has a bonfire going in his back yard, sending a towering column of smoke into the bare branches of the surrounding trees. With no wind to dissipate the smoke, it hangs like a flimsy shroud over the naked branches. The surface of the lake is flat calm and even without sunlight, the reflections of the houses and trees can be clearly seen. Closer to home, in fact no more than ten feet from where I sit writing this, silvery rain drops hang from the dark, bare branches of my fig tree. Nature's decorations. Nothing man-made can even compare with this display.

On a totally different note, I'm going to change the subject to remind all drivers to please take extra care to avoid any animals that you might encounter on the roads. Killing someone's beloved pet must be extremely depressing for both the driver and the pet owner. I happened upon just such an incident a couple of days ago. I was out driving my two Best Buddies, Sam and Dee, for their daily ride. Sam was up on my shoulders, between the headrest and my neck with his head right alongside mine. This is his favorite place to ride. Dee was sitting up in the doggie bed strapped into the passenger seat. It must look a bit strange from the outside and I've seen several people laughing and pointing at us. I sometimes wave back at them. Now, where was I? Ah yes, the accident. As we came round a bend I saw a car parked on the edge of the road with its hazard flashers on and a man with a phone held to his ear. His lady companion was pacing the edge of the road, obviously in distress. In the middle of the road I saw the battered body of a small black and white dog. There appeared to be no sign of life and the driver was obviously calling for help. On the opposite side of the road stood an elderly lady, very upset with her hands up to her face. There was nothing I could have done to help by stopping and the traffic both ways was starting to jam up, so I continued on my way. Which really is just as well. Had I stopped, I wouldn't have been able to hold my tongue. First of all, the driver should have been aware of the dog being loose and on the highway and should not have been traveling so fast that he couldn't stop in time to avoid it. Secondly, the owner of the dog was also partly to blame. No dog should be roaming, unrestricted in public. It's not safe for the dog, as was proven that day. And it's not safe for the public either if the dog is at all aggressive. There have been plenty of examples of dogs attacking children which might not have happened if their owners showed enough care and responsibility for their animals, to properly fence their property. Isn't there a law in Henry County which states that all dogs must be on a lead when outside the confines of their home? If there isn't, there should be. Please don't misunderstand me; I love all dogs and I don't blame them in any way for these unfortunate incidents. So please, dog-owners, stop and think what more you could do to secure the safety of your best friend. The love of a good dog is worth so much more than the cost of a few yards of chain-link fencing.

I was really upset by the accident and I cut our ride short to get home as quickly as I could. It was only about two miles but during that ride I counted five dead squirrels, a dead rabbit, two squashed possums and a dead cat. All those beautiful little lives cut short just because some inconsiderate drivers couldn't make the effort to avoid them.

KNEE REPLACEMENT SURGERY

A lot has happened in the last month or so, here at Swan Lake and I suddenly realize that I haven't written anything for anybody in quite some time. I've really been busy, not so much with the wildlife, although they, of course have still received their daily "treats", but with playing "nurse" to my wife, Millie, who had to have her left knee replaced. She had the right one done some five years ago, by the same surgeon. Well I'm happy to say that she is recovering well, still with a small amount of pain if she exerts herself too much but that is to be expected. She was able to walk around the nurses' station the next day after the op. with the aid of a "walker". She even found the walker unnecessary after a couple of days at home. To say that we were pleased with the outcome of the operation is an understatement and we both have the highest possible regard for Dr Scott Cahoon's abilities as a surgeon. He is also a caring, personable, easy to talk to doctor with a great bed-side manner. I would give Dr Cahoon a rating of 10 out of 10. With a full complement of patients in that section of the hospital, the nursing staff had their hands full with all the paperwork that had to be completed. Millie was discharged by the Doctor at around 8 a.m. but it was midday before we could finally leave the hospital to return home.

Since leaving the Hospital I have had to do the home nursing part of the program with help from a physical therapist (1 hour, twice a week) and a nurse (also 1 hour, twice a week) for three weeks. All the fetching and carrying helped to wake up the arthritis in my own right knee and I spent most of the time hobbling around with an elastic brace on my leg like the grumpy old man that I am. It hasn't been exactly a lot of fun for either Millie or me but it gave me a reason for being, I guess.

A few days ago we went to see Dr Cahoon for the post-op. visit. He was very pleased with Millie's progress and when she asked if she could drive the car yet, he replied, "Well, I don't know. Could you drive it before?" It was probably an old joke for him but it was new to us. Good one, Doc, I hope I haven't spoiled it for you. Since then she has made it a point to drive herself where ever she wants to go, even going back to Sunday School and Church.

Speaking of such, when the subject of an upcoming operation was discussed at the Sunday School, several of the ladies got together and made arrangements to supply us with meals for more than a week after Millie returned home from the hospital, to save me the trouble of having to cook. At first I was a bit hesitant about that but when it was explained that it would make them feel better to do something helpful and to be involved, I couldn't refuse. And I am so glad I didn't. Some of the good folks who helped us so much included Reeda and Lee Patterson, Starr and Robert Bogle, Bill and Ann Connerly, Anna and Lloyd Hamilton, Trina and Charlie Phillips, Don and Billie Newton, Cathy and Jim Gedhardt and last, but certainly not least, Jackie and Harry Stuckey. There were others too, of course and I want to thank everyone for all the support, love and prayers that we felt throughout this rather trying time.

The First Christian Church of Stockbridge really came through for us with a constant stream of visitors both in the hospital and at home bearing gifts, flowers, cards etc and most of all, their prayers. Preacher Jim has a wonderful and loving congregation and even an old "sinner" like me can feel blessed to know them and to

count them amongst my friends.

LOW WATER AT SWAN LAKE

It has been several weeks now that the water in Swan Lake has been really low. My poor old pontoon boat, still tied up to my sea wall sits, leaning over at about twenty degrees, on the hard muddy bottom. It doesn't look too happy there and naturally the afternoon picnics with the Kids have been postponed for a while. I'd like to think that the level will soon be allowed to rise back to normal but I know better than to expect that. The reason for the low water has been the repair work being done on the dam. It seems to be taking a lot longer than originally estimated but I'm sure that if asked, the powers that be would have several reasons why it is taking longer. As I understand it, it has been found necessary to install a siphoning system so that the water pressure on the dam wall can be relieved in times of heavy rains and to help the natural reduction in level managed by the spillway at the southern end of the dam.

I don't get the impression that many of the wildlife are enthusiastic about the idea. Big flat webbed feet work much better in water than on dry land and some of the food I throw out for the birds doesn't quite make it to the water. They're getting used to that gradually, but it is still an obvious effort on their part, to pick up all the scraps. Around and under the dock there is no water now and the dried mud bottom stretches out about thirty feet before it touches the water. The feeder box is now too high for Lucy or her three broken wing patients to reach so she now directs me to the area beside the sea wall which is the cleanest spot for me to drop their food. And "direct" she does. When she sees me approaching with the bucket of food in my hand, she runs along the sea wall bottom, squawking and honking at the top of her voice, to the area she has chosen. I toss the food down to her and she herds the three patients in to get their share. When they have finished eating they all waddle out to the water's edge and have a quick swim to settle their meal. If the sun is bright they then spend the rest of the day sunbathing and preening and getting ready for the next feed.

With the bottom of the lake showing up dry in so many areas, Big Daddy has become a little more subdued in his antics. He seems to think that his Lake is being taken away from him. A foreclosure perhaps? Whatever the reason, his attitude towards the other residents has improved considerably. He even paddles gently past Lucy's injured Canada goose sanctuary without upsetting the patients in any way. They can't believe what has happened to him and are obviously still a little wary of him. Who can blame them after the way he previously behaved around them? He still gets fed, of course, but nowhere near the dock. He and the other Canadas, Solo, Dodger and an assortment of ducks all get their treats around the bow of the grounded pontoon boat. Big Daddy generally waits until most of the food has been eaten before he starts chasing anyone and making a nuisance of himself but anyone can see that he has something on his tiny little mind and he just isn't putting his heart into it these days. Which is heartily appreciated by the other birds. I still can't decide whether it is the work being done on the dam, the low water level or could it be the fact that Spring isn't too far off and the only other unattached female swan on the lake is his grand-daughter. Now there's a scandal for the tabloids! Even the News channels on T.V. should be able to make something of that!

FULL POOL AT SWAN LAKE AGAIN!

It has been some time since I wrote about happenings at Swan Lake and I suppose the biggest piece of news is the fact that the work of installing the siphon system in the dam wall seems to have been completed successfully. The water is now back up to a normal level where the mud flats have submerged and my old pontoon boat is floating serenely at the bottom of my back yard. All the wild life seem to be much happier with this arrangement and this fact coupled with this extraordinarily early Spring has got them all thinking of establishing new families. Big Daddy has established some kind of relationship with his grand-daughter and they appear together on most mornings for their breakfast snack. Another pair, brother and sister I believe from the Southern end of the lake, also pay us the occasional visit but only when Big Daddy and his lady friend are absent. I haven't come up with a name for Big Daddy's new love yet; any suggestions would be welcome!

A few weeks ago I came upon a rather unusual situation and I've been meaning to tell you about it, so here goes. Now I'm not making this up, this really happened. I was sitting at this window, doing a little writing for the Times when, out of the corner of my eye, I noticed some kind of movement going on at the boat ramp on the opposite side of the lake. I went into the sun-room, overlooking the water, where I have an old pair of binoculars and, using them, I could make out a large collection of turkey sized black birds, gathered on and around the boat-ramp fence. This was something new and as I am always interested in what the wild-life of the lake are doing, I collected my car keys and drove around Lakeshore Drive to the end of the dam wall, close to the boat ramp and the Beach House. I parked the car about twenty yards away from the nearest perched bird and strolled over, somewhat cautiously I must admit, to see what the gathering was all about. I soon saw that these birds were buzzards of some kind with big, black, hooked beaks that looked like they could do some real damage to anything with meat on it. Three of the birds were down at the water's edge on the concrete ramp, tearing and ripping at something in the shallow water there and I began to think that I may have discovered a corpse. I slowly climbed through the fence, all the time conscious of the lethal, black looks I was getting from the other thirty or so onlookers packed on the surrounding fences and slowly approached the feasting area. I couldn't make out what the target of the bird's interest was until I shooed the diners away from their meal and found the torn up skeletal remains of one of the big carp which live in the deep water close to the dam wall.

There was no way to tell how the big fish had perished and I turned and retraced my steps back to the fence, still under the watchful gaze of all those evil looking scavengers. I stopped walking right beside the fence and I just couldn't resist it. The tension was almost palpable. I slowly turned to face the crowd and returned the stares for a few seconds. Suddenly I threw both hands in the air and let out the loudest and ugliest snarl which I could muster and the mood of the moment instantaneously changed from threatening to outright panic. There were big black buzzards crashing into each other on the fences and on the ground in their efforts to be the first to put as much distance as possible between themselves and this crazy creature who had disturbed their feast. Previously I had no idea that buzzards ate fish. Perhaps, to them, Swan Lake is their version of

Capt. D's (That's Captain Don's, of course!)

LUCY'S NEW VENTURE

Spring has gone and Summer is upon us and the wildlife of Swan Lake are settling in for some hot and humid weather in the weeks to come. We seem to have slipped from Fall, last year, into Spring, this year, with very little Winter in between and we've been riding a wave of seventies and eighties, touching on nineties, for some time now. The seasons seem to be all messed up and so far, the usual junior additions to the water-fowl population of the lake have been notable for their absence. In fact, the only new additions I have observed so far, are a family of six baby Canadas and their parents, who were crossing the road at the Northern end of the lake when I returned home from the last meeting of the Heritage Writers Group. They were scattered about on the road and I had to stop and let them get organized on one side of the road before I dared move ahead. The parents weren't doing much to guide them and I thought to myself, *Those kids need a Nanny!*

Lucy must have been out there somewhere, reading my mind, and the next time I saw the family together was about a week later, early in the morning as the Kids, that's my two little dogs, and I were going for our daily drive. The family was crossing the road to get to the water. Unlike the untidy crowd that we saw the first time, they were now formed up in a marching squad of three columns of two babies each, followed by the two adults bringing up the rear. A very neat and tidy little procession, with Lucy marching alongside in her contrasting, bright, white uniform. She was making some strange, ungoose-like sounds which I took to be her version of *Left, Right, Left, Right......*

She had the situation all under control and strutted along

with her head held high and her chest stuck way out. She knew she was doing a good job and was rightfully proud of herself. It was much safer for her charges to be in an organized group rather than strung out all over the road. Some drivers don't care about anything other than themselves and running over a few baby geese wouldn't cause them to lose even one wink of sleep. I had stopped the car a few yards away from the crossing area and when the road was clear I pulled away, waved out of the window and called out, "Well done, Lucy."

This new venture of Lucy's must have come about by the fact that her previous "patients" have all disappeared. She used to be the nurse for all injured Canada geese on the lake. I haven't seen B.W. (Broken Wing) or B.L. (Broken Leg) for a couple of months now and for the last two weeks, Lucy has missed breakfast with us several mornings. I still put her food in the box but I suspect that the Moscovies probably help themselves to that, once I go back into the house. Anyway, it looks as though Lucy, the Nurse, is adding to her qualifications by being Nanny to this family of young Canada geese. Obviously her duties also include those of Crossing Guard and Drill Instructor. It will be interesting to see how she copes with the situation when the babies take to the air.

Now that's a lot of responsibility for a senior goose. I don't know exactly how old she is but I've lived at the lake for eighteen years and she was here when I arrived. We've been friends for all that time and she still surprises me with her care-giving abilities and her energy. She really is "The Lady of the Lake", much more so than any one of those ill- tempered swans.

THE MAGNIFICENT, MELODIOUS, MELLIFLUOUS, MOCKING BIRD

I had never met or noticed a mocking bird before I came to America in the mid eighties. My first job was as a financial analyst for a Naval contractor in Crystal City, Virginia. One of the "Beltway Bandits." This entailed frequent visits to the Naval offices, just a block or two away. Relatively fresh from seven years spent in the desert of Saudi Arabia, Crystal City was more like a Concrete Jungle to me; the only "greenery" being the decorative trees planted along the sidewalk.

Spring was in the air one morning as I made my way towards the Naval building entrance, along with several other employees. As we approached I noticed that everyone was heading towards the far door, avoiding the closest of the two doors. I didn't see any sign saying

"Closed" or words to that effect so I went straight towards the nearest door. Out of the corner of my eye I was suddenly aware that many of the other people there had stopped and were watching me, with smiling faces as I approached the building. Skirting around a small tree I headed towards the door and was suddenly the target for a very irate and forceful little bird. I was immediately on the defensive, bending over and trying to shield my eyes, still hanging onto my brief case and shuffling as fast as I could towards the door. There were a lot of chuckles and restrained laughs following me as I finally managed to get into the lobby of the building, shutting out my winged adversary. "What on earth was that?" I asked the guard who issued a visitor's pass for me.

"Oh, that? That's our new Special Services Security guard. He does a good job, don't you think? I'm sorry about that, it's my fault, I forgot to put the "Closed" sign on the door this morning. There's nothing more defensive than a mocking bird. He's got a young family in that tree."

"Thanks for telling me; I'll be very sure to follow the crowd next time".

That little incident has been recalled many times when I've noticed a cat tearing across the lawn with a gray and white bundle of furious feathers hot on his tail. Size and species doesn't appear to concern the little guardian and just recently I saw two mocking birds "escorting" a red tailed hawk away from our corner of the lake. They don't appear to be bullies as I've never seen one attacking a smaller creature than itself and for that fact alone they deserve our respect.

Yet another one of the mocking bird's extraordinary talents is his ability to copy and sing just about any other bird's song. Often with more style and professionalism than the originator of the tune. I have one who occasionally entertains me with an impromptu song and dance act on the top of the pole, usually reserved for the hawk. He starts off with a beautiful medley of assorted bird calls, beak pointed Heavenwards, and then jumps high into the air, twisting and turning so rapidly that it is hard to follow, before he lands back on the pole in his original take-off position. He normally gives me at least half a dozen variations of this performance before he zooms away so quickly I begin to wonder if he was really there.

After he leaves the pole I often hear his songs coming down the chimney into the den where I am writing. Several times I have managed to get up quietly and go out through the sun-room to the back yard where I can see him perched on the chimney top, broadcasting his music to me and the rest of the world. He might not have many original pieces in his repertoire but I would put him

at the top of the charts for his performance, presentation

and poise.

(I just love alliteration!!)

LUCY AND HER TRAINEES ON PARADE

It has been over two weeks since we have had the pleasure of Lucy's company at the early morning breakfast snack. Lucy, as regular readers may remember is a large, pure white, farm-yard goose with nurturing tendencies. For several days I continued to put food in her box, just in case she decided to join us later but she didn't arrive to eat with us and the rest of the gang squabbled noisily over the extra rations. Actually, she could stand to lose a few pounds; she has more than enough fat on her to keep her afloat for quite some time. And then, the day before yesterday, I heard her familiar bellow coming from the other side of the lake. In the dim light, just before sunrise, I couldn't make out any details on the far shore but I could recognize that call anywhere. She still didn't make an appearance at snack time so I assumed she must have been getting food from someone else.

Yesterday, after all the other birds had gathered round and were nagging me to get on with the feeding, I noticed a small gaggle of Canadas turning the southern corner of our cove and heading towards us. Lucy stood out in her snow-white uniform, directing the small flotilla from the off-shore flank and they looked like a well trained group of Naval Cadets. Lucy must have been working them hard since she took over their family and they really looked proud of themselves and their instructor as they approached the gathered undisciplined mob in orderly fashion. Lines were straight and heads held high, beaks pointing directly ahead. It really was something to see and the crowd was highly impressed, moving out of their way as Lucy brought them to a halt right in front of me where I stood with the food pail.

"Good morning, Lucy," I called, and she replied with one of her somewhat less than musical screams which I took to mean, "O.K. Get on with it. You wanted to see what I was doing, so now you know. Let's eat!" Fortunately, it was also one of those infrequent days when no swans were present to cause trouble and after throwing out a generous helping for Lucy and her squad, I spread the rest of the food around so that the spectators also had a snack. It didn't take long for all the food to disappear and Lucy called her charges to order. The young Canadas reformed their squad and followed Lucy back around the southern point, headed to points unknown.

Unfortunately, this morning the young pair of swans arrived early and were looking for some Canadas to chase. They must have heard about the little show and breakfast party we had enjoyed yesterday and were determined to see that there would be no repeat performance. It's strange, isn't it? When I first came to Swan Lake I didn't understand why Swan Lake didn't have any actual swans. I guess that someone on the Board of the Association also felt we should have swans and they appeared a few years ago. They certainly make a beautiful picture as they cruise along like miniature old-time sailing ships. It's just a huge shame that they have such a mean disposition towards the other birds. They particularly dislike the Canadas and chase them away at every opportunity. Maybe the human race has set an unfortunate example. Perhaps if we all could learn to accept others of different nationalities, the wildlife might follow suit. I really don't think that's going to happen but I don't think it's a bad idea. In the mean time, as far as the swans are concerned, that situation reminds me of the old saying, "Be careful what you wish for!"

WHAT WONDERFUL WEATHER FOR WEEDS!!

A couple of weeks before this seemingly endless heat wave set in, I started to pay just a bit more attention to my long suffering garden. Since that little health episode which resulted in a short hospital stay last year, I have had neither the strength nor the dedication to do much about keeping the back yard up to the original standard. Back in the day (I love that phrase!)I have had visitors ask me if that was what an English garden looked like. Someone even suggested that I should be selling tickets for the tour!

Anyone seeing it today should be asking when does the safari start and which wild animals might we encounter on the trip.

I started to make a few inroads on the vast mounds of unwanted vegetation before the weather became so hot but along with the slightly cooler temperatures of Spring, my resolve melted when the heat began. It's strange really, that my body should react so severely to high temperatures. After all, I've spent most of my adult life in deserts and jungles around the world. I still have a strong dislike for extreme cold; if I never see another snowflake it will be too soon. But nowadays, any reading on my indoor/outdoor thermometer lower than 50F or higher than 80F is knocking on my discomfort door. Come to think of it, my few years in the Caribbean were probably the most accommodating, as far as the weather was concerned. I never even experienced a hurricane there and that's where they all seem to start. Of course, by the time they become fully blown hurricanes, the occasional storms have to leave the islands and grow into monsters.

Getting back to the original subject, according to the title above i.e. weeds. When the heat really started I couldn't do much more than force myself to cut the grass or what passes for grass. Each time I swore that I wouldn't wait so long before cutting it again and each time it was a major battle. As most of my grass is of the "crab" variety, like most weeds it thrives on just the very occasional shower and heat. I was tempted to stay awake one night to see if I really could see it grow but in the end I just turned over and went back to sleep.

I would have to say that crab grass is the number one weed in my yard but there have been several, previously unseen, weed types appearing this year. One of the most prevalent is a plant which bears miniature pea pods as seeds. I saw a few last year, before I became ill, but this year they were everywhere and waist high. The record breaker, as far as I am concerned was a plant which shot up in my bearded lily plot, close to the stump of an apple tree which I had cut down a couple of years ago. The leaves on this plant seemed to indicate that it could have been a member of the dandelion family. But I've never before seen a dandelion grow to ten feet high. It had a crown of dozens of tiny yellow flowers and I was just thankful that it wasn't a bean-stalk and that my name isn't Jack! Before I tore it up I took a photo of it, just to prove to myself that it really existed.

Another plant which has become a weed of the worst kind is one which I planted intentionally. When I first came to Georgia I met the beautiful Wisteria, growing and flowering in many of the local hedges and when I found a plant in the nearby garden shop, I just had to have it. And now it is everywhere in my yard and I just can't get rid of it. My garden swing is barely visible, the Forsythia bushes are totally covered with the vines and to make matters worse, it doesn't even bloom! I've tried every kind of weed killer, even such things as gasoline, bleach and rock salt to no avail. Of course, I have to be careful that whatever I use doesn't get into the lake water but it seems to thrive on anything that I put on it. So if anyone has any "Agent Orange", left over from the Vietnam War days, I'd like to hear about it.

IN PRAISE OF DOGS

With the arrival of Fall and slightly lower temperatures, we have been able to spend a little more time out of doors, even to the extent of charging up the batteries and going for an occasional boat ride. It was interesting to see the Kid's reactions when they first saw me taking the boat keys down from the key rack beside the back door. Sammy stopped dead in his tracks, ears pricked up and stared at me with those beautiful, big black eyes with his head tilted to one side. I could almost hear him thinking, "Are we really going for a boat ride?" It's been many weeks since we did that and a boat ride was long overdue, according to both of my Buddies. Dee was a little slower to catch on but when she picked up the vibes from Sam she went ballistic, running round in circles, tripping over her own feet and if her tail had been a propeller she would have taken off backwards. Neither of them had forgotten the routine and we were soon "All aboard!" For a short while we were able to forget those blisteringly hot days of Summer and we just cruised around the lake exchanging greetings with our many land-lubber canine friends.

At one point of our trip we passed by a house from which we could hear the plaintiff yelps and whines of at least two very unhappy dogs. I noted the location and after we finished the cruise and tied up the boat, I took my car and drove around the lake to see if I could locate the owner of the dogs. They were shut in a small, fenced off area on the side of the house, with no shelter from the elements and with half a pail of dirty water. Perhaps it was just as well that I couldn't locate the owner but I will certainly try again if I hear those cries for help. As far as I am concerned, no mistreatment of dogs is justified under any circumstance. If I can't do anything about it personally, I'll certainly make sure the ASPCA, Animal Control, PETA and the Henry County Humane Society all get to hear about it. People who have no interest in or respect for any creature other than themselves should not be allowed to own pets. Why would they want them? Just to tie them to a tree in the back yard or to leave them all day, and all night too in a fenced in kennel which probably hasn't been cleaned for weeks. I'm sorry if I have offended anyone with these remarks but if you are, then you are the one they are aimed at. "If the cap fits.....wear it!" as my old Grandma used to say.

Looking back over my life there have been very few periods when I didn't have at least one dog in the house. I never had a dog that lived outside, they have all been part of my family. Even my Police Dog, when I served three years as a Dog Handler in the Royal Air

Force, on active service in both Egypt and Africa, was as much a true friend and companion as any human being. We saved each other's lives on several occasions and I never really got over it when he died. Rex was thirteen years old when he went and was senior in rank to me. He had lived a full and useful life in the Service and I still miss him. There have been several dogs in my life since I left the R.A.F. in the fifties and everyone has been special to me. These days Sam and Dee, my two "Best Buddies" make up for the love and care which was lost when all their predecessors came to the end of their short lives. They took over the job of looking after the Old Man very well and I would be totally lost without them

SAMMY'S SOUP

It is now the middle of the last full week of October and, according to the weather forecast, there are only a couple of days left of this incredibly fine Fall weather before the cold sets in. That means we definitely have to go for a short cruise this afternoon so that the Kids can eat their dog food on the boat. That really is the only place they will eat enough Kibbles to constitute a full meal. In the house they pick and choose a few pieces but they really want some of what I'm having and I always have to leave them just a taste.

One evening last week, when the wind was blowing a little too strong for a comfortable boat ride, Millie and I decided to have bowls of soup for dinner. One of our favorites is Vegetarian Vegetable from Ingles.

In addition to vegetables, it contains the capital letters of the alphabet, in pasta. Now, I realize that many readers of this column will disbelieve what I am about to tell you but please, try to keep an open mind. I'm not making this up. It would take quite an imagination to do that and that's something I don't have. Anyway, back to the story...................................

Sammy, as usual, was sitting at my feet, under the dining table as I was eating my soup. I could feel his eyes on me and it was clear that he was reminding me to save him some. I said to him, "It's O.K. I won't forget you. But I don't think you're going to like this. There's no meat in it, just vegetables. If you don't like it, just say so." I put the soup bowl down on the floor close to him and watched as he sniffed at it suspiciously. "Well," I asked, "Don't you want it?" He turned his head away from the bowl slowly and stared straight at me. I could feel the rejection in his eyes. Floating together in the center of the bowl were the pasta letters NO. I could hardly believe what I was seeing. I said to Millie, "I know Sammy is incredibly smart, but this is unreal" as I pointed out the soup bowl on the floor. She laughed and replied, "You don't really believe that he moved those letters to make the word 'NO' do you? It's just a coincidence." Well, maybe it was and maybe it wasn't............what do you think?

I still believe that all dogs are much more knowledgeable than we give them credit for. I know Sammy understands everything I say to him. He just chooses to respond to those suggestions and ideas which interest him and he ignores anything else. I've never given either of my Best Buddies any obedience training as I never intended for them to be "working dogs", like my Police patrol dogs, back in my R.A.F. Service days.

These two have been allowed to develop their own personalities, unencumbered with any rules or restrictions except for not being allowed to roam freely outside the confines of our property. When we are outside the fence, even as far as getting into the car, *their car,* by the way, they are on leads. This is for their safety. Inside the car the leads come off.

Dee is a totally different character. She loves everyone and gives big, sloppy, wet kisses to anyone who will allow it. She also chooses not to hear any of my suggestions which don't interest her but, in her case, not much of what I might suggest does. In some respects, she is very much like my wife. I call it "Selective hearing"..........there I've done it now! Ah well, I'm accustomed to sleeping in my recliner. With Sammy curled up alongside my legs it's really quite comfortable.

CRS and TMB.

Since my Best Friend, Durant Godwin, aka "Auto Doc" was diagnosed with lung cancer I have got into the habit of taking him, and anyone else who happens to be visiting him at the time in his "shop", an ice-cream cup from my favorite grocery store, Ingles. The treatments which he has been receiving have affected his taste and he says that the ice-cream is about the only thing which tastes good. Anyway, it's good to see him eating something. This morning was no different and when I stopped in there with my insulated cold bag, only one other visitor was there, our other close friend and another "Don". To try not to confuse the story, I'll call Don by his nick-name, "Lobby."

Sitting in Doc's tiny, overcrowded office, half deafened by the roar of the space-heater and the country music blaring from the radio, conversation was all but impossible. But that's the way Doc likes it. After we had eaten our ice-creams we collected up the empty plastic cups, for me to deposit them in the garbage can outside on my way out, and then I poured myself a cup of Doc's excellent coffee. I think it's the well water that makes the difference but Lobby calls it commode water. He doesn't really like coffee and he has a strange sense of humor. Just before I sat back down with my coffee, I turned the volume knob down on the radio, which lowered the background noise considerably. I thought I had got away with it but before I reached my seat, I heard Doc say, "While you're there why don't you mess with the radio?"

"What'dya say?" I replied.

"You know what I said"

"You're right, I think I've heard you say somethin' like that on previous occasions."

That just earned me a dirty look which I chose to

ignore. Now that the only noise was coming from the space heater in the adjoining room I figured I might be able to get some help with my main problem which had been bothering me for the past week.

"Okay, guys, I need some help with a non mechanical problem. If you remember I told you I had bought a 2 ½ gallon gas container a couple of weeks ago and I didn't realize it had some kind of fancy safety spout on it. It's so safe, in fact, I can't even get the gas out of it!"

"I don't remember hearing about that," said Lobby

"Nor do I," said Doc. "And there's nothing wrong with my memory"

"So you're saying that my memory is lousy? I don't know what you're talking about!"

"See, you've already forgotten what we were talking about!" said Doc, pointing his finger at Lobby.

"So what are we talking about?" I interjected.

"Well, you should know – you brought the subject up, didn't you?" Lobby said.

"What subject?" I asked. "Just tell me what we're talking about."

They both looked at me as if I'd lost my mind and there are times when I'm pretty sure I have. From conversations with other, shall we say, mature people this is not an uncommon problem so if it happens to you, don't let it upset you. It's certainly not worth getting your blood pressure up for and you'll forget all about it after a couple of minutes. But it is aggravating and if you think you might be suffering from CRS (that's Can't Remember Stuff) or the advanced version TMB (Too Many Birthdays), just remind yourself, you're not an isolated case.

XMAS 2012

Time is passing so quickly these days, but it's hard to believe that Christmas has come round again so soon. All the mad hustle and bustle at the stores as millions of people race to rid themselves of their savings to buy those all important gifts, many of which will be in the long lines after the Holiday, to be returned, resized or replaced. All good, clean fun, I suppose and I'm sure the retailers are laughing all the way to the bank. But really, is that what Christmas is all about? Isn't this supposed to be the time when we celebrate the Birthday of our Saviour? I've seen very little reference to that in the un-ending, ever-repeating commercials on television but like everything else these days it's all about the money.

As a child growing up in war-torn England in the late thirties, our Christmas wasn't much different from any other day. Church services recognized the

importance of the day of course and if you happened to

have a pine tree in your yard you were lucky. Most

people couldn't afford to waste money on a Christmas

tree and I don't think that fake ones had been invented

then. Everything was severely rationed so there was very

little with which to make pastries, cookies (called

biscuits, in England), cakes and other goodies which we

take for granted these days. But somehow, by a miracle

of home economics, Mum always managed to produce a

Christmas pudding with custard as a dessert after we had

finished the roast chicken. Television hadn't been

invented then so after the big meal of the year was

finished, we listened to the radio and sang along with any

carol-singing we could tune in to. Just being together as a

family and not getting bombed (that's using the true

meaning of the word!) meant more than any store-bought

trifle and was certainly more than enough reason for us to celebrate the Birthday of Jesus. We were fortunate that Dad's work as a Borstal Officer did not require us to live in a city, where the destruction was intense but we still had to put up with the occasional raid when the German 'planes went scurrying back across the channel after bombing London, chased by the R.A.F. Spitfires and Hurricanes. Any bombs left over from the raids on the city were dropped randomly as the Nazis crossed the coast, to lighten their aircraft for a speedier retreat. And we were right on the coast in a place named Portland, just south of the port city of Weymouth.

About two years into the war, Dad was offered a transfer to another Borstal on the East coast of England, known as Hollesley Bay. It seemed like a good idea at the time. We moved and then found ourselves in a very rural environment. The war, at that time had not affected

East Anglia very much and was much quieter than Portland. That didn't last long as we were on the flight path for the Flying Bombs, or Buzz Bombs which were rocket powered, pilot-less aircraft filled with high explosives. It became a nightly custom to stand at the front door of the house and watch for the exhaust flare being followed by a stream of tracer shells. Every time the anti-aircraft batteries down at the beach scored a hit, there would be an almighty explosion in the sky, followed by a resounding cheer from the neighbors who were all doing the same thing as us. The cheer was immediately followed by the sound of slamming doors as we all ducked inside to avoid any falling shrapnel. I spent a couple of Christmases doing that and I have to admit there wasn't much in the way of Christmas celebrations going on, at the time. But we all knew who to thank and praise for our lives, once the dust settled.

I wanted to tell you about the one Christmas present I received which I never forgot and somehow I got lost in my memories of that time. When D-Day finally arrived Dad and I stood at the front door watching hordes of heavy bombers, some towing huge gliders as they headed across the open water of the North Sea. The beach was only a couple of miles from the house. As they flew overhead I commented, "Don't they look great, Dad?" and he said, "They certainly do but it is a crying shame that so many young men will die or be injured, when they get to where they're going."

That Christmas Dad gave me a solid wooden model of a four engine R.A.F bomber, which he had made, like those we had seen going to France. It was beautiful and it sparked my interest in model aircraft which lasted for many years.

So, please have a wonderful time this Christmas

but please remember the reason for it all. Without Him,

we wouldn't exist and don't let any of us forget that.

CUSTOMER SERVICE.

Six years ago, I retired from a Customer Service position with a light engineering company after thirteen years of dealing with customers requiring accuracy down to one thousandth of an inch in everything we produced for them. No excuses, and I soon learned the basic rules for being a good Customer Service Representative, or CSR.

Rule No. 1 Say what you do and do what you say.

Rule No. 2 Do unto others as you would have them do unto you.

Those rules apply to just about any business and service which has customers, clients, etc. Over the last few years it has become evident that these rules seem to be coming obsolete at an alarming rate. Recorded and or computer generated inquiries have done nothing to improve the situation and being put "On Hold" recently by a machine for at least five minutes was just about the last straw with me. The day is fast approaching when my telephone will be replaced by a smoky fire and a wet blanket and the computer will be much more useful as an anchor for my old pontoon boat! However, all is not lost. There are some folk who still believe in and practice those two basic rules and I would like to say "Kudos" to those fine people.

Number one on my short list would have to be my best friend, Durant Godwin, aka Auto Doc. In spite of having to battle the ravages of radiation and chemo for the treatment of his lung cancer, he still manages to complete any auto repair work which comes to him. When I try to get him to "Take it easy!" he just gives me a dirty look and says "The customer needs his vehicle. That comes first."

A close second would have to be the ladies of the Stockbridge Tag Office. They are so polite, friendly and helpful they even make the whole process of paying vehicle taxes a pleasurable experience instead of a painful one. The Tax Commissioner is to be commended on his choice of staff; they all do an excellent job.

Next on my list are the two Doctors in my life. Dr William Jackson of Britepoint Urgent Care and Dr. Barry Dix of Southern Heart Specialists. They each have truly wonderful staffs who really connect with their patients. I have never been kept waiting beyond my appointment time at either of their surgeries. I've had experience of other medical practitioners in the past and believe me, these two are special.

Fifth on my list of exemplary service providers is the Berry Hill Pet Hospital. It has only been during the past year that I have discovered Dr Richard S. Pfouts (the

"P" is silent) and his pet hospital at the Airfield on Millers Mill Road, Stockbridge. Dr Pfouts has two charming and knowledgeable assistants, Julie and Carla, who work wonders with the patients. My two Best Buddies, Sammy and Dee love to go there, if only for a toe-nail trim. They consider it a social visit rather than something to be frightened about and I don't feel like I've been stabbed in the wallet when we leave.

Number six on my list is the local branch of Ingles, the grocery store on Fairview Rd. Ellenwood. That place is almost like a second home to me. I consider the staff as my friends and it is a great feeling to go into the store and be greeted as a friend. It is a very rare occasion when I have had to go into another store to find something "special" and I hope nobody sees me. I've lived in this area for eighteen years now and I've been an Ingles customer from day one. The friendly, polite and helpful attitude of both the staff and management makes a shopping experience memorable.

So there you have it, there are still people who recognize the meaning of "Good Customer Service". I know it is unrealistic to expect that kind of personal attention everywhere in this age of advanced technology but it sure does a heart good to be greeted with a "Hi, Don, how are you?" and a handshake.

AMISH AND PUPPY MILLS

Recently my wife, Millie, was out shopping and noticed a book for sale which she thought might interest me. It is titled "One nation under Dog." It was interesting to start, being an analysis of the increasing awareness and interest in this country of the importance of dogs and cats, not just as pets but as members of the family. The author discussed his researches in, what he terms to be, a fascinating cultural phenomena. I wasn't particularly fond of his style of writing but he did open my eyes to a lot of facts and information of which I was previously unaware.

The fact that there are now so many more thousands of households with pets than there were fifty years ago should not really be that surprising. There are also many more thousands of households to accommodate them. This all means that there is a need for puppies and kittens far greater than the natural process can supply. So-called Puppy Mills have sprung up in several parts of the country. According to this book, Lancaster County in Pennsylvania is one place where breeding dogs are kept in filthy and disgusting conditions and just reading about it brought tears to my eyes. I was always given to believe that the Amish people are good, God fearing people with respect for themselves and other creatures. Apparently, that's not necessarily true. If there is money to be made by selling puppies to pet stores, they readily put their consciences "on hold" and hope that God is not watching them as they torture and abuse dogs to assuage their desire for the mighty dollar. They and others like them make me sick. Puppy mills are not restricted to that area of the country. They can be anywhere. Sometimes a hand-written notice on a garden gate might indicate one but mostly, it seems that the breeders supply pet shops. Perhaps we could make a difference in the situation if all prospective pet owners would stop buying that cute little puppy in the pet store. It really is worth the time and possibly a little bit of inconvenience to visit the local pet shelters and see if you can't find just the right dog for you. It's not hard to do. The hardest part is, once having chosen your new companion, having to leave all the others behind. I have two such "rescue dogs." One came from Henry County and the other from Clayton and they are now, and always have been, the greatest blessings I could wish for.

Having a dog (notice I didn't say "owning") is a big responsibility and should not be undertaken lightly. If you are not prepared to tolerate the learning period during the early years and the additional expense then you might want to think again. After all, you will be taking on a new family member. And please, never give a puppy, kitten or any other pet to a child as a Birthday, Christmas or any other kind of present without first getting the Head of the Household's express permission. Too many pets can have unfortunate endings to their short lives that way. Both of my Best Buddies had unhappy beginnings – Sammy, who is now busy snoozing quietly under a throw rug on "our" recliner was abandoned in an apartment and Dee, currently asleep on a faux fur rug on our bed with her head on my pillow, was seriously abused. I think they would agree that their lives have definitely improved. And that's the way it should be. They give me so much love and companionship I don't even want to consider what life would be like without them. Just a couple of days ago I had a bad bout of indigestion after dinner (and I'm the cook!). It was a very sharp pain and I excused myself from the table and went to lie down on the bed until it passed. As soon as I stretched out, I heard Sammy's footsteps as he climbed the set of steps at the foot of the bed and he snuggled in beside me. He was crying softly, like a baby. He was letting me know that he was worried about me and I had to reassure him that everything was going to be alright before he relaxed and we both took a short nap.

ODDS AND ENDS

Well, here we go again. It's been so long since I have made time to sit down and write to y'all, that I have almost forgotten how to use this beat-up old lap-top. It literally is held together with duct tape: quite appropriate when you consider that I generally write about my wild-life friends, particularly ducks. I haven't spent a lot of time with them over the last few weeks except for giving them their breakfast each day and, since my friend Doc finished with his chemo and radiation treatments, I've had to give them their snack around 7 a.m. It's nearly always before daylight these days so, although I can't see them very well, I can hear them and I recognize most of their calls. That's the only way I know who is there and who isn't. My reason for feeding them so early, before daylight, is so that I can get on the road to Conyers to pick up my friend Doc and take him to his workshop on 155, just North of 138. He was told by his Doctor not to drive while he was going for treatment so another good friend of his and I have been taking it in turns to drive him to work in the mornings and back home to Conyers again in the afternoons/evenings. Doc's other good friend, Jimmie, takes him for his medical appointments, the next one being tomorrow afternoon. We all have our fingers crossed and are praying hard for a good report. He seems to have improved over the last few days and is more like the old Doc. Hard headed and speaks his mind, fully convinced that he is right! Most of the time he is right. But nobody's perfect, I keep telling him. He just ignores me, so lately I've been calling him "Rock", instead of "Doc." I said they must have used him as a model for Mt Rushmore.

With all this running around, dealing with the day-to-day "SNAFUS" that seem to occur daily, yard work, taking care of our two old cars, making sure our two four-legged Kids want for nothing and trying to stretch a dime into a dollar, time has been slipping away from me at an ever increasing speed. Just glancing out of the window at the old pontoon boat, reminds me that the batteries need charging and I need to do something about the plywood deck which is getting soft in places. It's been about six years since a good friend of mine helped me to replace the deck and he has since moved to S.Carolina. It all just seems to be a bit much for me these days along with the garden which resembles a patch of overgrown scrub land. I'm reminded of that famous movie line - "I'm too old for this stuff!"

Last week I joined two of the ladies of the Heritage Writers Group in a book-signing evening at Moye's in McDonough. Naturally it rained – if it wasn't for bad luck I wouldn't have any luck at all! Of the few customers who came into the store only a couple showed any interest in what we had to offer but the evening was not entirely lost. This was my first visit to a Moye's store and I was totally amazed at the incredible variety of items stocked there and the very reasonable prices. I wish I had known about Moye's before Christmas. In future, when any gift-giving occasion arises, I'll head straight for Moye's. It will save a lot of running around, when just about anything and everything a person could possibly want is all on display in one place. All this and a pharmacy too. And something else which saved the evening for me was the exceedingly high level of customer service. Even though we were not there as customers, the staff were all helpful and charming, turning what could have been a disappointing wash-out of an evening into a very pleasant experience. "Kudos" to the Management and Staff! That's it for now, so until

next time – 'Bye.

COMMON SENSE, COMMON COURTESY

Recently I have had to drive from Stockbridge to Conyers and back again on a fairly regular basis. These trips mostly took place in the early part of the day, before sunrise and quite often in heavy mist, fog and sometimes pouring rain. My old car, a 1996 Chevy Lumina, still runs great (my BFF, Auto Doc, has cared for it since new) and all the lights work as they should. I see no reason not to have them turned on when poor visibility demands it. Unfortunately, not everyone seems to take the same view. I gave up counting the number of vehicles with no lights on in inclement weather conditions and many more with only one headlight working. Isn't there a law regarding this? We seem to have them for everything else. But apart from the legal aspect, surely it makes sense to drive with lights on, low beam of course, when visibility is poor, not only to help the driver to see where he is going (common sense) but also to let other drivers know that he is there (common courtesy).

The two "commons", both "sense" and "courtesy" seem to be sadly missing in today's techno world and I don't relish the thought of a future without either.

Thinking about the use of lights on vehicles, how about the turn signals? How many times has some self-centered idiot driving in front of you, suddenly made a turn with no warning. Or used a turn signal? Turn signals on vehicles are there to indicate to other drivers an intention to deviate from the road ahead and should be used (common sense). This will enable the following driver to apply his brakes gently, if necessary, instead of having to come to a screeching halt to avoid the turning vehicle ahead, and possibly causing a chain-reaction pile-up behind (common courtesy).

Of course, if your lights, signals etc. have burned-out bulbs in them you can flick your switches as hard as you please, your lights will still not work. (common sense) It doesn't take much to check them out but do it in your driveway. Turn on all the lights and walk round the vehicle and note any which do not light up. Apply your turn signal, say, to the right and check if the turn signal lights are on, both front and rear and then do the same with the signal on for the left turn. The only lights which might be a little more inconvenient to check, if you don't have a helper handy, are the brake lights. Unless you happen to be a giraffe, it's difficult to step on the brake pedal and see if the brake lights come on at the rear of the vehicle. One way to check is to back the vehicle up to any convenient window where you can see, in your rear-view mirror, the reflection of the rear of the car. Apply the brakes. The red brake lights should be lit up on both sides of the car – not just one side; both sides.

Now I don't claim to be the best driver in the world but I do know what I see on the roads and that is a lot of drivers who either don't know that they have faulty lights or who don't care. (common sense and courtesy – lack of!) I have established a weekly ritual to keep my vehicles legal. On Sunday afternoons, after my post lunchtime nap, I check the oil, water and lights on my car, my wife's car and my old '84 Dodge truck, even though the truck, like the driver, doesn't go too far these days. It's not fool-proof, I know, but it's better than not checking at all. Anyway, I can't afford the tickets I might get if I didn't, at least, try. Once you have determined which lights need attention, either fix them yourself or do as I do – go to your friendly local mechanic. I guess I'll have to find a new one now that the best mechanic I've ever known, my friend Doc, is incapacitated.

RETURN TO THE WILD

It is now almost four years since I first wrote about my experiences of living on Swan Lake, just outside of Stockbridge and it seems that lately, I have wandered a little from my original subject matter. Some of my readers have graciously reminded me of that so now I'm getting back on track.

My first column, dated 10th June, 2009 was titled "My Friend The Cardinal" and concerned the recovery of a beautiful red bird which had flown into my sun-room window and crashed. This was brought to mind two days ago when a red winged black bird suffered a similar accident. I heard the "thump" when he hit the glass and rushed outside to find him laying on the thick uncut weeds that represent my lawn behind the house. Now I know why I had felt no urge to cut them; they provided a soft landing spot. He was laying quite still with his beak open and barely moved when I bent to pick him up very gently. He laid in my hand, eyes open but not moving and at first, I thought he may have killed himself but then I felt a slight pressure from his claw, gripping onto my finger. Slowly the pressure of the tiny talons increased on my finger which was under him and I knew he was regaining his strength. With his beak still open, I carried him around to the hosepipe and allowed just the slightest dribble of water to moisten his beak. He blinked the eye that had been staring at me vacantly, turned his head to face straight ahead and shuffled his feathers slightly to make his nest, in my hand, a little more comfortable. I really didn't want to let him go until he was fully recovered as there are more than a few hungry feral cats in this area, so I carried him over to the bird-bath next to the lake. There was only about half a cupful of water in the bottom and plenty of dry surrounding area where he could sit until he had the strength to fly again. He seemed to be quite content with his surroundings and I was just standing there watching him, ready to extend a helping hand again if he was going to fall. For a second or so my attention was suddenly distracted by a loud squawk from the lake. It was a mallard duck who had decided that he needed some attention too and was demanding a snack. I looked at "Red Wing" who was sitting up and taking notice and I told him to just hang on while I went to get the duck some food. It is only a couple of steps to the shed where I keep the food and a few seconds later I returned with the snack. Red Wing, in the mean time, had decided to take to the air again. He had flown away but not before leaving a small deposit, against a future visit possibly? Since that episode I have noticed many more red-wings in the back yard. Perhaps my Red Wing has spread the news that they are welcome here and will receive good food, love and attention. I like to think that he will return but then, I'll never know. They all look the same and if one seems to stay a little longer than the rest of the flock, that's just coincidence, isn't it?

My wild-life friends and I still enjoy our early morning breakfast gatherings even when the temperature is below freezing. Before dawn breaks, the "quackin'", "hootin'"and "hollerin'"from the lake tell me that it is time to stop watching the "no-news" news on the television. I struggle out of the recliner and Sammy stretches out under the blanket to keep my place warm for me. He draws the line at coming outside to feed the ducks in the kind of weather we've been experiencing lately but that will change soon, we hope. This crazy mixed up Fall/Winter/Spring season has got, not only the wild-life but also the plant life totally confused. It feels like Mother Nature has taken a vacation. But then, she deserves one. She has been looking after us all for a very long time.

LUCY'S LOST LOVE

I haven't seen much of Lucy recently and, being a concerned friend of her's, I decided to call someone who I just knew would be able to give me an update on Lucy's whereabouts. Pam, the Duck Lady of Swan Lake, answered my call and when I mentioned Lucy she told me that she was spending all her time these days, minding Pam's little flock of Pekins. At one time, several years ago, Lucy had had a mate who was not particularly fond of children. He used to chase them away, whenever he found them paddling and splashing around at the beach area. One morning, his body was found floating up against a boat dock. Yet another unsolved "crime" in Henry County? Anyway, Lucy took a long time to get over her loss and for many nights after it happened, I could hear her calling forlornly for her mate. Eventually her grief was redirected towards her new life purpose which was to help the less fortunate among the various breeds of waterfowl on the lake. Any bird, duck or goose which was having a hard time surviving, came under the watchful eyes and care of Nurse Lucy. Even the swans were a little intimidated when the cripples were feeding and Lucy was on guard. Eventually, Lucy discovered that Pam's little haven for ducks, both tame and wild, was the ideal location for a body guard/nurse and she moved in, with Pam's happy consent. Having so many other birds around to watch over, a series of ponds, waterfall, ramp to the lake and a lakeside duck house she soon appeared to have finally put thoughts of her previous mate behind her. But not for long, apparently.

One evening Pam heard a faint tap, tap, tapping sound coming from the window which overlooks the duck pond at the top of the waterfall. It was Lucy, very gently pecking at the glass. Pam couldn't see anything on the window which might have been attracting Lucy so she quietly went outside and around the side of the house to the pond. From her new vantage point Pam soon understood what was happening. At that time of day the light was just right for the window pane to be acting as a mirror. Lucy was seeing her own reflection and thought that there was another goose, just like her, inside the house. Remembering her long-lost love, she didn't want to scare the stranger away by appearing too aggressive but she really wanted to catch the newcomer's attention. It was obvious to Pam that Lucy was hunting a memory of times past when she and her consort would cruise the lake together, enjoying life and making a charming contribution to the pristine beauty of the lake. If only another white male goose would fly in and settle on the lake – that would be the answer to a lot of prayers!

Pam said that this incident also taught Lucy a new trick. That goose is incredibly smart and picks up on anything which she can use to her advantage. She must have taken notice that when she had pecked (kissed?) the window, she had drawn Pam's attention to her. Now, when she decides that it is time to be fed, she rattles her beak on the window pane and lets loose with several of her trumpet calls, which, according to Pam, will awaken the dead! It really would be nice if she could find a new mate although, at her age she just might not want to settle down again. She might be too accustomed to being her own boss and regard any newcomer as an intruder. But it would be interesting to see!

SPRING HAS FINALLY SPRUNG

Many, many years ago, when I was a young boy, and I got into mischief, somehow my Dad always seemed to know about it. Every time I asked him how he knew, he would always answer "A little bird told me!" Well, just the other day I was in my recliner, dozing in front of the T.V. while the evening News was on when I suddenly had the thought that it must surely be time to put out the humming-bird feeders. The thought was so strong, overpowering the old so-called "News", that I opened my eyes. The first thing I saw was a beautiful little Hummer, hovering outside the den window, looking straight at me. "O.K" I whispered, "I'll get a new feeder for you tomorrow", and away he flew, message delivered! Early the next morning, I put the harnesses and leads on the Kids and we set off for Home Depot to see what kind of feeders are in style this year. Last year's feeder was stained so badly that I couldn't bring myself to use it again. When I found the section that contained bird feeders I was surprised and gratified to see that there were more spaces than feeders on the shelf, indicating to me that many other Hummer fans had heard the call! Looking over the remaining assortment, I decided on a 12 oz model with four feeding stations in the shape of yellow flowers. At first I thought that maybe the birds wouldn't like it but they haven't stopped visiting it since I filled it and they certainly seem to be enjoying their new snack-bar.

Yesterday I finally picked up the last of the pine cones which, thanks to the hail storm on the 18th of last month, were covering my little back yard. I certainly could not have picked them all up without the help of my beat up old "grabber". That has to be one of the most useful tools in any garden. I still have a burn-barrel full of cones to dispose of and when a fishing boat passed by in the lake as I was working on them, I called out to the two young men in the boat and offered them all the pine cones they might want - "For Free!" They declined my offer, laughing, and called back that they had plenty of their own.

Looking out the window beside me, I see that there is not a breath of wind on the water, which is like a huge mirror. This is the view I fell in love with when I first came to Swan Lake. The reflections of the trees on the far shore, starting to fill out with the buds and new leaves now that Winter is finally behind us, I hope. And there sits my old friend the hawk, this time on the canopy over my pontoon boat, surveying the property for an early morning snack. As fat as he is, I'll wager he hasn't missed too many meals lately.

Thinking of the boat, I went aboard yesterday to put the two batteries on charge. With the change in the weather we should soon be able to resume our afternoon picnics on board which the Kids think is the best. Maybe they'll get back into the habit of eating their Kibbles again and lose some of the weight which they gained over the winter from sharing my meals. I had hooked up the charger and turned to get back on shore when I noticed some ripples on the water, between the boat and the sea-wall. I kept still and watched and after a few seconds I saw the water moccasin poke his head out. With his mouth against the wall he slowly wriggled along, apparently finding something to eat there. Maybe some of the duck's breakfast had stuck to the cement. Anyway, I wished him a "Good Morning". He turned his head, looked straight at me, opened his mouth and flicked his tongue. I guessed he was telling me, "Get lost!" and without hands and fingers, that was the only way he

could say it.

A LAZY WIND!

With the outside temperature at 34F and the wind a steady 20 mph that's what I consider a Lazy Wind. It doesn't take the time to go round a person, it just cuts straight through. Feeding the wild life at dawn is quite a chore but it has to be done. They still need their early snack, whatever the weather and there has been an interesting development lately which I was keen to observe this morning. For the last two years, when the other birds have been fussing over their "treats", a small flock of dainty, little black ducks with white bills has been hovering on the outskirts. They would never join in and would even fly away if I tried to gently throw some food in their direction. Recently, the small group of black ducks has been getting a little bolder and even coming close enough to grab a few morsels, left by the others. I was a few minutes late getting out to feed them this morning and when I arrived at the preferred feeding place, in front of my old pontoon boat, the small black ducks had gathered together, "front and center". They must have agreed amongst themselves that it was now time to take a chance and to grab their fair share. Fortunately, for them, the swans were absent and the other birds didn't seem to mind the newcomers crashing the party. I would still like to know their name, but no luck so far.

On my way to the feeding site I encountered another one of our local characters who I haven't seen for well over a year. The water moccasin who used to sunbathe on the rear of the boat had been doing whatever snakes do in the bearded iris bed close to the water. I really had no argument with whatever he was doing but he must have felt guilty about it. As soon as I was within a couple of steps from him, he dashed out in front of me wriggling and twisting and dived straight over the sea-wall into the lake. That little performance got the sleep out of my eyes in a hurry. Two more steps and I would have been right in his way and he may have thought that I was trying to interfere with his escape plan. He was quite a big fellow; I estimate his length to be around three and a half feet but he disappeared quickly into the depths of the water. The birds didn't seem to be too concerned so the rest of the breakfast gathering went off with no more incidents.

Do you remember my telling you about a white goose which I named the Artful Dodger for his ability to avoid Big Daddy, the older male swan by diving and turning away, under water and by getting out of the water to walk on the land, which Big Daddy really hates to do? Well, I have to admit that I made a big mistake. It seems that He is actually a She but short of getting on much better terms with a goose than I really would like, how could I know? It all became clear when I noticed, on the end of one of the islands, easily visible from the road , what looked like a white garbage bag caught up in some weeds. I told my friend Pam, the Duck Lady about it and she told me that she had investigated from her paddle boat and it was not a garbage bag but Dodger sitting on a nest. Wouldn't that be great, if we have some home-grown white geese on the lake? But who would the father be? The only other white goose who lives here is Lucy! Could I have made a big mistake there too? Or perhaps a stray goose, returning home from a wild weekend with the boys, dropped in for a drink and a nap and then the rest is history, as they say. Yet another unsolved mystery of Henry County and who said that this isn't an interesting place to live? I still find it hard to believe that

I have made a mistake about Lucy's gender. But what do

I know? I just feed them.

HOW HIGH THE MOON?

It was a beautifully clear evening and the crescent moon glowed brightly in the star laden sky. A visiting friend had been bragging to me about the number of miles his truck had traveled with no major repairs and I couldn't help comparing his odometer reading with that of my old Chevrolet Lumina car.

"Right now," I said, "My old car has 236,632 miles on her and still going strong. I just need another 2,268 and I'll be happy".

"How come?" asked my friend.

"Well, I heard somewhere that it's only 238,900 miles to the moon and I want to be able to say that my old car has been as far as the moon!"

"Just one thing," he said "If you go all that way, how are you going to get back?"

"It shouldn't be a problem," I replied, "I'll just coast home, it looks to be all downhill from there!"

Poker-faced he looked at me, tapped the side of his head with his finger and said, "You know, Don, you ain't right!" as he cranked up his truck and drove away shaking his head.

The following evening my wife and I were watching the so-called "News" on T.V., each with a dog cuddled up alongside us, when suddenly we were thrown into the middle of WW111. At least that's what it sounded like. "What the heck is going on?" I said, or words to that effect, as I was suddenly engulfed in two small bundles of trembling black and white fur, doing their best to hide from the racket. I struggled up out of my recliner, thinking that at any moment the house was going to collapse. The banging and clattering was incredible as I looked outside and saw all the chunks of ice hitting the back yard and my old tool-shed. In all my travels I had never experienced anything like that. It was a hail-storm that I won't soon forget. When it eased off, I went outside to check on the cars and my old Dodge truck. They all have to "live" outside because the garage is used for "other things". From the front they all looked fine and I heaved a premature sigh of relief. The truck was faced away from the house and the two cars were faced towards it, all with no immediate evidence of damage. Chunks of ice lay everywhere and I had to be careful where I put my feet. Eventually I made it to the far end of the cars and then I saw that my old Lumina had suffered the worst. The back window was completely destroyed and there were millions of tiny pieces of glass mixed in with the ice.

"We should have started off for the moon a little sooner," I thought, "It might have been a bit safer up there."

Anyway, it could have been a lot worse. The old truck has a cracked windshield but that just adds to its old country charm and all three of the vehicles have developed "dimples" in their skins.

The ice had barely melted when we started being swamped with roofing repair offers. In the mail, on the 'phone, even in person while I was checking the outside of the house in daylight the next day. Fortunately, we had some work done on the roof a few years ago and were very pleased with the results so a quick call to Rhillips Roofing and Siding put our house back on Mr. Phillips' schedule. Just something else to brighten my day. And I thought retirement would be boring! No such luck!

MY BEST FRIEND

It is now the 6th May, 2013, three days since Henry

Durant Godwin, known to many as "Auto doc" or just

plain "Doc", passed away. He fought a good fight for

over a year but cancer finally took the life of the man I

have called My Best Friend ever since I met him, almost

eighteen years ago. To me he was the younger brother I

never had and, as a brother, I loved him.

The first time I met Doc was shortly after I arrived

in Georgia from N.Carolina, to take up a new job in

Decatur. I had made the trip in my ancient Dodge truck,

towing my small outboard boat. Maybe it was the long

drive towing a boat, that overtaxed the truck but for

whatever reason it had decided that enough was enough

and, one day it refused to start. I tried to find a mechanic

to fix it and one even came around to my house on his

motorcycle to see what he could do. He tried but eventually gave up and told me that if it was possible to get it running again there was only one man that he knew who could do it. He gave me Doc's 'phone number and I called him. He answered the 'phone with his signature greeting, "Auto Doooarc". I told him about the truck and my address on Swan Lake, Stockbridge which is about five miles from Doc's shop. "Leave the key under the front mat tomorrow and I'll take care of it." he said.

The next day when I came home from work the truck was gone from the front yard. I wondered if I had made a mistake, entrusting my beloved old truck to a stranger who I hadn't even met yet. I needn't have worried. I called Doc again and he told me to come and pick up my truck, the following day which was a Saturday. I thought he meant that he couldn't fix it and wanted to get it out of his way. My wife took me to Doc's shop on Hwy 155 the following morning and, front and center, sat my Dodge. Doc came out of the office and said, "That's a good, old truck, you got there. The timing gear needed a little work but she runs like a good'un now." He gave me the key and a bill that was just a fraction of what I had expected. Right then, I knew that I had found a good honest mechanic and my opinion of him has never changed except to say that the "good" part has long since been upgraded to "incomparable." He has never met a mechanical, electrical or hydraulic problem that he couldn't overcome that I know of and many of his local mechanic friends would call on him for advice when they had problems. He could repair just about any machine you can think of, from a vacuum cleaner to a weed-eater to a Caterpillar tractor. If it had an engine of any kind, it was no problem to Doc. He also had a heart as big as all outdoors. At first, he came over a little gruff and expressed himself, sometimes, in somewhat colorful language which he must have picked up during his four year stint in the U.S.Navy but he would always help a customer who might have been unable to settle a bill at the time. He sometimes extended credit to the wrong customers, even to some he called his "buddies", who never paid what they owed him and the pile of old, unpaid, workshop orders on his desk testifies to that.

Doc's son "Bud", daughter-in-law Penny and daughter, Nadine were with him when he passed and I had spent a few hours with him two days before. He was so weak then that I doubt if he knew I was there but at least I was able to tell him "Good Bye" and that I loved him.

Doc had quite a large circle of friends and we all took turns in caring for him at the house after he insisted that he wanted to be at home. At 78 I'm not able to handle much in the way of nursing duties so most of my efforts went into driving him around once the doctors had taken him off the chemo and radiation treatments and told him not to drive.

There is so much more I could tell you about Doc but he was really a private kind of person who didn't open up much about his past. I don't think he would like me to share, with everyone, the little he told me about his life before we met. So I'll leave it there but I will say that the world and particularly our little corner of it, has lost a truly great man. Life will never be the same without him.

A LABOR OF LOVE

A little over 20 years ago, a young man named Bill Woods moved to Henry County with his wife, Diane and family. Bill had served 4 years with the U.S.Navy, from 1968 to 1972 and had traveled to many places in the world, primarily in the Far East. Bill and Diane have two children, Elizabeth and Nick, both native Georgians and they live, with their beautiful 14 years old Boston Bull Terrier in northern Henry County. Bill is a self employed automobile glass technician which is how I came to meet him. During the hail storm which we experienced in March, the back window of my old Chevy Lumina was smashed and I asked my best friend, Auto Doc, for a recommendation for a good glass man. Doc immediately told me to call Bill, and gave me his number. Doc even guided me around to Bill's house, in the hope that Bill would be there. He wasn't but his son, Nick was there and we chatted for a while. During our talk Nick happened to mention his father's hobby and asked if I would like to see it. Not knowing what it was I agreed. I wasn't in a hurry.

Nick led the way into an area at the rear of the house and down a slight slope to a wooden door in a frame, displaying a 'Welcome' sign. I was a little hesitant as I remembered Doc and his son, Bud were sitting in their truck in the driveway and I didn't want to leave them waiting for me.

"I can't stay long, Nick" I said, "Doc and Bud will need to get going."

"That's O.K. Just take a quick look and you can come back when Dad's here. I know he will want to show you this, himself."

Stepping through the doorway, I found myself on a

smooth, flat rock pathway leading down to a stream where the sun was sparkling and flashing on the water. The wooded areas on both sides of the water are covered with a carpet of bright green moss and exotic plants and ferns hug the banks. Looking at the pathway, on which I was standing, I asked Nick, "How did this path get here? There seem to be thousands of flat rocks of all sizes, shapes and colors."

Nick smiled and said "That's Dad's hobby. He collected and laid all these stones himself, but you really need to have him tell you the full story. Maybe you could come back some time and see it all?"

"You can count on it!" I replied as I dragged myself away from what looked like a little piece of Paradise.

A few days later, Bill had found a used window for my car; new ones were not available for my 1995 car;

and came to my house to install it. We talked for some time and he invited me to visit his house again to see the entire project. We set a date and I could hardly wait. Call me an old softy if you like, or maybe it's my second childhood kicking in, but I couldn't help thinking that there was something magical about that place. It was so quiet with the sun's rays filtering through the tall trees, lighting up the musical chimes of the water flowing along the creek.

On the appointed day, I was right on time when I next called on Bill. The weather was perfect and we sat in his kitchen, talking and drinking coffee. At last it was time to get started on the tour. We headed for the 'Welcome' door and along the path inside to another world. Nothing could displace the calm and serenity of that haven of peace. Even the birds' songs seemed somehow muted and no wind disturbed the atmosphere.

"So tell me, Bill, how did you get started on building this beautiful place?" I asked. Bill told me that when he and Diane decided to move to Henry County he had told his wife that he wanted a house with some water on the property in a peaceful area away from traffic and the 'hubbub' of modern life. Diane searched diligently until she found the perfect place. They moved in and a couple of years later, remembering the magnificent landscaped gardens of the Orient which he experienced in his youth while serving in the Navy, Bill started to collect flat rocks that he could place together to form a path. That was over 21 years ago and the project still continues. Bill has gathered many thousands of flat rocks over the years to place on his paths, wearing out three wheel barrows in the process. He has built, all by hand, over 400 yards of flat stone paving meandering through a lush, green oasis, each stone carefully selected and fitted, by hand, into place. He never breaks a rock to make it fit, he knows what he needs and he searches for just the right stone until he finds it. I asked him, "Where do all these rocks come from?" expecting him to say that he buys them, in bulk, from some landscape garden shop.

"They come from wherever I find them." he replied. "I carry my wheel-barrow in my truck and when I see a likely place for rocks, like a ditch or some wild country, I search the area. Over the years I guess I've cleaned out most of the suitable flat rocks in Henry, Rockdale and Clayton counties!" He grinned when he saw the amazed look on my face. I just couldn't imagine the amount of patience a project like this would require. He mentioned that he had found a large rock in the land bordering his "project" which he would dearly love to have as an accent piece but it was too big and too heavy for him to lift. I said, "Why don't you just break it up in smaller pieces, perhaps you could blast it?" The look on Bill's face showed me that I had made a serious mistake with that suggestion. "That wouldn't do, now would it? Breaking a rock, whatever the size, would only leave sharp edges and all my rocks have rounded edges, smoothed by weather and running water. Nature has supplied enough rocks for me to continue building my paths without smashing anything up. All I have to do is find and collect them." In addition to the paths there are hundreds of feet of retaining walls faced with flat rocks, a magnificent picnic area and several benches situated at focus points along the way. All of this is Bill's handiwork and he has no intentions of ending it soon. He's in it "for the long haul", as they say!

Just being allowed to visit this incredible work of art is a huge privilege, as far as I am concerned. Bill spends every minute of his spare time working on improving and enlarging his dream. Photographs cannot do it justice, each shot only shows a small section and each section needs the presence of all the other parts for a visitor to feel the full impact of the achievement.

Consider the thousands of hours, over approximately twenty years, that Bill has spent creating a masterpiece. Most of them on his knees, selecting just the right rock that would fit exactly with its neighbors to create his walk-ways. And then doing it again an untold number of times. This truly has to be acknowledged as a genuine Labor of Love.

A SNAPPER SAVED

One morning last week, I was taking Sammy and Dee for their morning drive and instead of going out of our driveway and turning left, for some reason I decided to turn right. This took us down to the northern end of the lake. As we approached the bend in the road around the lake's end, I noticed something in the center of the black-top which, from a short distance, looked like a crumpled up black garbage bag. One of my pet peeves (and I have several!) is garbage which has not been placed where it belongs, i. e. in a garbage container. Anyway, I slowed down with the intention of picking it up and disposing of it when we returned to the house. Pulling up alongside the object, I opened the car door and stepped over a really unpleasant looking snapping turtle. I had never seen one, up close, before so this was a real find for me.

There were no other cars around so I figured I would take my time and examine it for a few minutes. I carefully picked the turtle up and was surprised at how heavy it was. The carapace, just a fancy word for "shell", was all black with hard ridges and looked like some weird kind of sci-fi battle tank. I turned it over to get a better look at the occupant, who really didn't appreciate having his sunbathing session disturbed and he let me know it by trying his best to snap my fingers holding his shell. I was holding him with my fingers well back on the sides so he couldn't reach me with that ugly beak but that just put my fingers in range of his back feet which were well armed with a set of toe-nails like teeth on a back-hoe! With my curiosity satisfied, if not fully, I held onto that snapping and thrashing monster as I danced around the back of the car with him fighting like a demon all the way and placed him, not too gently, on the lake side of the road, where he could easily get down into the water. Before I released him he expressed his "Thanks" by squirting water, at least I was hoping it was just water, all over the front of my jeans. There were no other people around to witness this encounter but my Kids, Sammy and Dee, were barking their heads off in the car, thoroughly enjoying the spectacle of their Dad, hopping around the car, holding onto but trying to stay away from a very angry snapping turtle. My only consolation was the thought that at least he didn't get run over by a car or truck. Not that time, anyway.

We continued our ride with both of my Kids giving me a good "sniffing". Sammy decided not to climb up around my neck where he usually likes to ride. As we approached the exit from the Swan Lake subdivision onto Swan Lake Road, I noticed something laying in the ditch, right at the junction. I had to stop at the Stop sign and I looked over into the ditch where a beautiful, adult female deer lay, dead. I couldn't see any signs in the grass verge where a body might have been dragged and dumped in the ditch. I could only assume that some-one had been going too fast through the Stop sign and hit the animal as it was crossing the road. Just because a driver was in too much of a hurry to get home that night, an innocent creature lost its life. The body stayed there for several days before it was removed; perhaps as a notice to drive no faster than your Guardian Angel can fly!

"UH OH, IT'S A CROW!"

Mr. Danny Phillips and I were sitting on the concrete benches, at the bottom of the yard, next to the water, solving some of the world's problems, while we watched the last few nails go into the roof repairs. That hail storm in March really tore up my property as it did many others and it was a great feeling to know that all would soon be right again. At least until the next time! Danny is the owner of Phillips Roofing Co. and he was explaining some of the technicalities of the job, most of which went straight over my head! Well, it would, wouldn't it, being a roof? Anyway, he was talking away and suddenly I heard someone say "Uh Oh" from right behind us. Danny was talking and didn't pay any attention to it so I thought, maybe, that either I imagined it or my neighbor, Barry, was trying to play a joke on us.

I didn't look round and a couple of minutes passed when the voice again said "Uh Oh" more forcefully than before, demanding to be heard. This time I said, "Hold on, Danny," and I turned and looked behind us, almost into the beak of a big crow, perched on the top of our chain-link fence.

Up close like that, he really appeared huge. I hadn't even heard him arriving there but he seemed to be quite at ease, listening in to our conversation. "What's up with you?" I asked. He gave me a blank stare and tten repeated his "Uh Oh" just as a Blue Jay dived on him from the adjacent pine tree. The Blue Jay was soon joined by another and between the two they managed to disturb the crow enough that he finally let out one more "Uh Oh" and took off across the water.

I saw the crow again this morning, while I was outside picking up pine cones and preparing to cut my grass. He was sitting on the top of my sea-wall fence and he appeared to be watching the antics of the martins who nest in the cracks in the sea-wall. I keep thinking that I should block those holes with mortar to make it look good. But then I think, "Well, if I did that, where would the martins go to raise their families? At least they know they are safe and will not be disturbed in my wall."

I stopped picking up cones and took a short rest, sitting on the bench which Danny and I had occupied yesterday. The crow would watch the martins flitting over the water and occasionally picking a tasty insect off the surface and then turning his head to look at me. He did this for several times and then, as though he had figured it was his turn to show off, he jumped off the fence top, swooped low over the water and dipped his feet in before climbing away to sit back up on the fence in his original position. He hadn't quite caught onto the reason for the maneuver, i.e. to catch something to eat. He seemed to think it was to wash his feet. He did this several times, each time checking with me to see if I was watching. Finally, wanting to get on with my chore, I called out to him, "Hey, I gotta go. Call me back when you get it right, O.K.?" At that moment, the blue jays appeared. With a quick glance at them my new friend, the crow, launched himself from the fence and with blue jays chasing him from both sides and a final, loud, "Uh Oh" he headed, at top speed, for the safety of the tall pines in my neighbor's yard where the rest of the big birds hang out.

I'm sure I will be seeing him again soon and I'll let you know if he has started catching insects off the lake as the martins do. Or is he just trying to start a new "Clean feet" trend amongst the flock.

RETURN TO "SERENITY"

On the second Sunday in June, I had the pleasure of returning to "Serenity," the incredibly beautiful garden owned by my friend, Bill Woods. I had arranged for a small party of interested members of The Heritage Writers Group to accompany me and we arrived there at 2 p.m. The weather forecast for that day was the usual Summer-time prediction of scattered showers and some sun and I was praying really hard that the rain would hold off for a couple of hours. It did that – just, and we all enjoyed and appreciated the serene wonder of the place. To realize that it was the result of one man's dedication, and love for Nature over a period in excess of twenty years that created such a work of art, is truly inspiring and I know that many of us were seeing the garden as the basis for children's stories, perhaps with movies in mind.

As we all congregated back at the picnic site after walking the flat-rock pathways along the creek and over the bridges, the showers started up, but with shelter from the umbrellas and the trees, nobody's spirit was dampened. The rain didn't last very long and, somehow it even heightened the sense of tranquility and peace while we enjoyed socializing and the provided riparian refreshments which consisted of sparkling grape juice, substituting for wine, and an assortment of cookies.

That was certainly an extremely enjoyable Sunday afternoon and on behalf of the Writers Group I wish to thank Bill, his charming wife, Diane, son Nick and daughter Elizabeth for allowing us to share in the experience of "Serenity."

While there, I was talking to Nick about modern electronics and how I had purchased a new Sony DVD player. I had tried to read and understand the instructions but being totally stupid when it comes to anything hi-tech, the DVD player was still in it's box. Nick immediately offered to hook it up for me and the next day he came to my house. It took him all of two minutes to complete the job, without even looking at the instructions! In addition to his electronics skills, Nick is an accomplished guitar player and singer and his art-work is perfect for book illustrations. I'm going to keep that in mind when I next have a book to publish.

Meanwhile, back at the lake, the wild-life still keeps me amused and at home. I really miss my feathered friends and my Kids (dogs) when I have to leave for any reason, although the greeting which I receive when I return is almost worth it. Last week I had to go for my monthly checkup to the heart Doctor and the Kids had to stay home. The weather is too hot to leave them in the car for any length of time, even with the engine running and the A/C on. When I came home, about one and a half hours later, the Kids were fine but I had missed a wild-life happening. Barry, my good neighbor, told me that he had seen a parakeet flying around his back yard and asked if I had seen it. Now Barry's not the type who would hallucinate over a thing like that and I know he doesn't drink. So I guessed that he had been taking a nap on his deck out in the sun and had probably dreamed it. Anyway, there was no sign of a parakeet out there then. The following day the 'phone rang and it was Barry. "Get outside quick, Don," he said, "That parakeet I told you about is out there again!" I quickly hung the 'phone up and tried to hurry, quietly, outside to the back yard. And sure enough, sitting on the top rail of Barry's garden swing was a golden headed bird with a greenish gray body. I couldn't say if it was a parakeet; it didn't look pretty enough to me but when it took off and shot across

Barry's yard to my little magnolia tree, like a flash of

bright green lightning, I had to agree that it was

something special. It could be someone's pet bird that

escaped it's cage but it certainly seemed to be quite happy

being free.

SWAN LAKE BABIES

This elongated Winter/Spring has certainly caused some unusual happenings in the Natural world, if Swan Lake is anything to go by. It seemed to take forever for the seasonal flowers and shrubs to bloom and when they did, it seemed to be all over in a week or two. My giant Snowball bush, outside our front door, made at least three attempts to burst into the usual avalanche of blossoms before finally it made it. It was a spectacular but short-lived show when it happened, only lasting a week or so before all the snowballs were melting into a brown, smelly mess on the ground. Definitely unusual. I've just about given up on having a beautiful flower-filled Summer this year and, of course, old age has quite a lot to do with that. Over the Winter my joints decided that they had been abused enough over the last 78 years and that it is time to just "chill out." If I could just get my

neighbor to keep his hedge trimmed, instead of leaving it

to grow, out of control, over my property, things would

be a lot easier. But, enough about that.

Just as much as the plant life was confused over

the last few months, so were the various forms of wild

life, in and around the lake. By now we should be seeing

many family outings among the ducks and geese. So far I

have only seen one duck family with five babies and a

single young Canada goose with no apparent parents. For

a while there, I thought that maybe the reason for the

poor attendance at the early morning breakfast sessions

was that the birds were busy nest making and sitting on

eggs. Only a dozen or so ducks and geese were regular

breakfast customers for the past three months, but

yesterday and today we had at least fifty to sixty birds

gobbling down the Ingles dog food which I supply for

them. They don't get much but it's better than nothing. Throughout this lean period for customers at breakfast, the male swan, Big Daddy's off-spring, invariably showed up to hone his bullying skills. I did manage to catch him a glancing swat with an old broken boat paddle one morning to try to make him behave but he just ignored me and kept on chasing the geese. It really is a pity that just one big bird with a bad attitude should have so much power that he can do anything he wants to with the rest of the flock.

This morning he managed to corner Dodger, the white goose, in a bush overhanging the lake from a neighbor's yard, on the other side of our little cove. Poor Dodger was caught up in the foliage and couldn't free himself for several minutes. Meanwhile Big Daddy junior, pecked on him mercilessly while Dodger was screaming at the top of his lungs. If I could have reached the scene of the "fight" in time, I would have slapped that swan silly. It only lasted a few minutes before the screaming stopped and Dodger escaped from the bush. He wasn't really hurt but he was still letting out an occasional screech as he stalked off across the yard, head held high while Junior was still in the water struggling to get free of the bush himself. He finally made it out into clear water and paddled back to our side of the cove where his mate had appeared with two brand new baby swans. The babies are really cute, looking like two white fluffy tennis balls with long necks. They had eaten some of the dog food which was left over from breakfast. The food was soft as it had been soaking for a while and they seemed to enjoy it. So that will be another two beaks to feed which will help to keep me poor but happy!

THE BIG BLUE BOMBER

One morning last week, I had been "working" out in the back yard and a few drops of rain started to fall which was enough to drive me indoors again for a brief water-break. It was just one of those "pop-up" showers that the weather man likes to talk about which can either amount to nothing or a deluge. That was my excuse for a few minutes rest time and I sat down on my old recliner, sipping on a glass of iced water. Seriously, it was only water and I was just getting up to go back outside when there was an almighty "thump" on the side of the house. Almost simultaneously, a large dark shadow flashed past the dining room window. I struggled out of the recliner and hurried to the sun-room door, just in time to see Big Blue, the big blueish-grey heron which lives and nests at the top of the neighboring pine trees. He swooped down low in a tight turn around the corner of my house and raced straight for the lake. This was a very strange behavior for him; I had never seen him flying so low, close to the house. That still didn't explain the noise I had heard of something hitting the outside wall. I went on a short inspection tour and discovered a fairly good sized dead bream, about ¾ pound, laying about 5 feet away from the side of the house. The siding had just been replaced a couple of weeks ago, as a result of damage caused by the hail storm in March.

There was no additional damage to the siding and no indication of what could have caused the sound of an impact. Obviously, the fish had something to do with it so I deduced the following chain of events.

That morning, Mrs Blue had asked her husband, Big Blue to pick up a nice fish for lunch. Mindful of his obligations to his family, Big Blue set out on a fishing trip to the southern end of the lake where some kingfishers had tipped him off about a good fishing area. When he arrived there he met up with several other herons on the same quest. A friendly contest soon developed to see who could catch, not only the most but the biggest fish. Time slipped away from him, he was having too much fun with his friends. When he realized he was going to be late, he hurriedly squawked a brief farewell to his friends, grabbed the biggest of the fish he had caught, leaving the rest behind, and took off for home. He decided to take a short cut and instead of flying out over the lake he reckoned it would be faster to fly over the houses. He had forgotten the fact that roofers were busy on several of the houses in that neighborhood and still weighed down by that big fish he was carrying he couldn't gain much altitude. Threading his way through the tall trees surrounding many of the houses, he was preparing to make a low approach over my yard when a loud explosion came from a roofer's nail-gun directly beneath him. Startled, he dropped the fish and in trying to catch it again, swerved into the side if the house. The collision shook him up badly and it was all he could do to pick himself up and get airborne again. He heard me coming to investigate so he didn't stop to retrieve his catch but flew off unencumbered by the weight of his fish.

So how about that for a piece of detective work. Or should it be "a piece of defective work?" Anyway, he probably had to pay for his sins when he got home. I wouldn't have wanted to be in his shoes (?) when he had to face the family with no fish. As for his catch, I picked it up and dumped it back in the lake. It probably fed a whole family of turtles.

I last saw Big Blue heading out across the lake in a

south easterly direction. He may have been going back to

the fishing hole or perhaps it would have been quicker to

just pick up something at Captain D's. Or maybe he just

kept on flying in search of a quieter life in another State.

FIGS AND FLATS

It's that time of year when the fig tree, just outside
my window has now out-grown the harsh pruning which
it received the year before last and is now covered in figs
of all sizes, from pea to golf ball size. Two days ago I
was working on the new lap-top computer, trying to
understand the mysteries of Windows 7, when I looked
up and through the window I saw a squirrel, sitting on the
roof of the lean-to shed, not six feet away from me,
holding a large ripe fig in his mouth. He appeared to be
really pleased with himself and I got the impression that
he was showing off for my benefit. He stayed there,
staring at me, for a couple of minutes before he stood up
and strolled to the edge of the roof and jumped back into
the tree.

It was then that I took a harder look at the tree and

noticed that there were several ripe figs in view and I knew that it was time to start some selective picking. I must admit that I have a severe case of fig fever and picking them means one for me and one for the collecting bowl. They are just so juicy and sweet that it's hard to keep from eating them all. I took some of them to the Breakfast Club this morning and the members also seemed to like them.

Of course the birds will be getting their fill soon; I've even seen a humming-bird sticking his long, slender beak into a ripe fruit and sucking on the juice. Naturally, like anything else edible in my yard, the wild-life has "dibs" on it all. But I know they will leave a share for me.

Now I have a true story I would like to share with you. Over the weekend, on Friday, I was driving in my old Lumina along Hwy 138 through Stockbridge when I heard a loud "pop." I didn't pay it much attention at first but then the ride became a little rough and I realized that I had a flat tire on my driver's side rear wheel. There wasn't much I could do about it there in amongst all that traffic so I just decided to drive on to the house anyway, going no faster than twenty m.p.h. I realize that I probably upset some drivers who were in a hurry and I apologize to them. Anyway, to cut a long, uncomfortable story short, I finally made it back to Swan Lake and home.

I really wasn't sure how I would handle the dilemma as my back, which was operated on a few years ago, won't allow me to do the bending down necessary to change a wheel. My wife, Millie, provided the answer. Just the previous week she had taken out a membership in AAA. Now that we no longer had Auto Doc to turn to when we had car trouble, she thought it would be a good idea. And she was right! I called on Saturday morning and was told a mechanic would be in my driveway to change the wheel, in thirty minutes. He was there in exactly thirty minutes and had replaced the blown out wheel with the do-nut spare and was gone ten minutes later. No charge! He was a very personable, polite and efficient young man.

Later that day I drove the car to my usually reliable used tire outfit where the man put replacement tires on both rear wheels. He said the previous tires were dry rotted out. Now guess what happened when I took the Kids, (my two little dogs) for their morning drive on Sunday. That's right! On the way back from Ingles, the tire on the driver's side rear blew out again! I wasn't about to try walking home with two small dogs, as hot as the day was, so once again I drove home on a torn-up tire, only this time I was followed by two motorcycles.

They made no attempt to pass me and when I turned into Knoll-wood Drive, the entrance to Swan Lake, one of the riders pulled up alongside and said, very politely, "Excuse me, Sir. Do you know you have a flat tire on the rear wheel?" "No kidding!" I said. "I thought the ride was a bit rough." I smiled as I said it and he said "We just wanted to make sure you were O.K. Can we do anything to help?" "That's O.K. I live just the other side of the lake and I'm pretty sure I can make it from here. But thanks for caring." He waved and they both roared off. If they happen to read this I'd just like to say, "Thanks again, guys. You're a credit to the motorcycling fraternity!"

BLACK LOOKS FROM BUZZARDS

A few days ago, early in the morning, I had to go for my blood count checkup at the heart doctor's office and I was backing carefully out of the driveway, looking both ways, of course. Looking in the opposite direction to which I intended to go, I saw what appeared to be a large black mass rolling around on a front lawn about a hundred or so yards away. That was before I had my new glasses which really make a great deal of difference. Anyway, curiosity killed the cat, as the saying goes and will probably get me too in the end, but I just had to see what it was, up close. Seeing those stories on T.V. News lately about black bears being in neighborhood back yards, I thought I might have a close encounter with one right here. So, of course I couldn't resist being a little late for my blood-letting to find out what was happening.

As I got closer, the black mass broke up into individual pieces and I could then see that it was a party of seven black buzzards. They didn't seem to be afraid of the car or me, as they continued their breakfast, cleaning up a dead possum that I had noticed laying on the side of the road, the previous evening. So they do have their uses. The stares that they gave me as I drove up right alongside them let me know that I wasn't really welcome so without disturbing them any longer, I turned the car around and carried on with what I set out to do in the first place.

Thinking of birds feeding, I reminded myself that the humming birds had not been emptying the feeder as they used to. When they first came calling I had filled the feeder with my own recipe of sugar water with a drop of red food color but they didn't seem to want that anymore. My neighbor, Barry, told me that he hadn't seen any around his feeder either, although he had seen them on the red honey-suckle in the hedge between our back yards. I began to wonder if my feeder was too old so I bought two more of a different design. One of the new feeders came in a boxed kit which also contained two bottles of ready mixed "nectar", with the admonition "do not add water" on the instructions. I opened one of the bottles and sniffed it. It gave off a really strong, sweet, syrupy odor and was scarlet in color. I didn't think those delicate little birds would go for anything that strong but I left the feeder hanging on a hook just outside the window for a couple of days. A couple of hummers dropped in for a taste but quickly left again. One even stopped in mid-air before they went. He stared at me through the window and I could almost hear him telling me what I could do with the food in his feeder.

Yesterday, I decided to change the liquid in the

feeder back to my original home-made variety. When evening arrived, the first hummer looked a little surprised when he must have noticed the change in color from a dark red to a dusty pink. He took a sip, just to see if it tasted O.K. and then sat there for quite a few seconds, slurping it down. It obviously suited him just fine and I fully expect him to return this evening for a repeat order!

Well, it looks as though it won't be long now before the birds and squirrels will have plenty of sweet stuff to eat from the fig tree which has grown so big that it blocks out most of the view of the lake from my window. I really will have to do some serious pruning, early next year, to get it back in control again. In the meantime, it is full of marble sized figs which will be delicious when they are ripe. I just hope the wild-life leave some for me.

HUMMING BIRD BALLET

It certainly is a nice break from the "pop-up" showers we were having on a daily basis that were less like showers and more like a Biblical event. Several times I caught myself looking at the old pontoon boat, wondering if I could build a house on it with enough room for the wife and I, two dogs and several other creatures. The hard part would be deciding how to find a male turtle as opposed to a female and the same question would apply to several other choices we have around the lake, including the humming birds. I couldn't take them all, of course, but I just had the feeling that I ought to at least try to help out.

This break in the weather, even if only for a short time has brought me down to earth again and for a total destruction of my fantasies, I have sold the boat and trailer. I haven't told the Kids yet. I'm not looking

forward to that task. That is if they don't know already.

I'm certain they can read my mind. It doesn't matter

whatever or wherever I think about doing or going, they

are always at least two steps ahead of me. That should

tell me that either they are way too smart or I'm

incredibly stupid....Duh!

The trailer has gone but the boat is still tied up to

the sea-wall at the bottom of the yard. I guess the Kids

think that they never got to ride on the trailer so that

doesn't matter but when the boat goes I'm sure I will have

a lot to answer for. I'll have to tolerate at least a week's

worth of "sulks" and hiding under the bed episodes, if I

know those two. "C'est la vie!" as a Frenchman might

say.

Getting back to the main theme of this column,

(and I have to scroll back to the beginning to see what

that was!) the hummingbirds who frequent the feeder hung just outside the window where I sit when I'm typing, have come up with some really classy dance performances lately. Generally there are only one or two feeding at the same time. There are four small bell-shaped feeding points and most of the times they are worried by a yellow-jacket or two. They dodge around, chasing or being chased by the insects. They don't seem to be upset with having me right alongside, watching them. I guess by now, they think I am just some part of the local scenery to be ignored. The other evening, at dusk, they started a new routine. Four birds arrived at the feeder within seconds of each other, one on each of the feeding stations. They started to feed and then, as if on cue, they all moved to the right, one space and continued feeding again. This went on for several seconds and then suddenly the "dance" changed directions and went in the opposite direction. There must have been some kind of signal because nobody bumped into anyone on the 'changeover' and everyone seemed to be getting a good share of the food. Perhaps this performance was some kind of defense mechanism against the yellow jackets who certainly didn't seem to be interested in joining in. The little dance continued in this fashion for several 'changeovers' when suddenly they each went their separate way. This performance was repeated several times; 'encores' perhaps? I still haven't figured out the reason for these antics; do they have humming birds in Texas? Maybe it's their version of Square Dancing.

My favorite time of day is the early morning when there is just enough light to see where I'm going and I feed the ducks, geese and swans. One thing has been missing lately, though. No early morning bird song. It's as if the birds are scared to open their beaks in case they get drowned by a "pop-up" storm. I and the wild-life will

be so thankful when the seasons "straighten up and fly

right" again.

DINNER TIME SQUIRREL

The figs have just about all gone now with just a few small marble-sized green ones left so I doubt we will be having many more visits from our customary dinner guest. Over the last few weeks, while the figs were ripe and plentiful on the tree, just outside the window we have had a visiting squirrel who stops to look at Millie and I as we are eating our evening meal. He stays for a few minutes, watching us, and then springs off the lean-to roof back into the tree. We can watch his progress as he goes from branch to branch, searching for the biggest, juiciest fig that he can find and then he bounces back onto the roof to show off his find before taking it back to his nest for dinner. We will miss our little visitor at dinner time but I can still see him every morning at the bird feeder, sharing the seed with the birds and throwing some down onto the ground where there are usually at least half a dozen ducks waiting to get his scraps.

This certainly seems to be the season for ants this year, at least it is in my yard. Aside from the numerous mounds in the so-called lawn and even a nest of them in my old burn-barrel, I found where they had even invaded my poor old 1981 Dodge truck, which very rarely gets used these days. It really needs a brake job but I still like to have it ready to go so about once a month I crank it up and let it run for a while just to keep the battery charged and the fluids flowing. Anyway, a couple of days ago, I decided it was time and jumped into the seat, put the key in the switch and, wouldn't you know it, it wouldn't start. I'm used to that now though. When it stands for any length of time I have to lift the hood, remove the air-cleaner and drop about a thimble-full of gas down the carb's throat. Crank it again and away she goes! This time was a little different. When I got back out of the truck, after the first attempt, I felt something tickling my arm. I looked down and my entire right arm was covered in millions of black ants. That got my attention and between the flapping arms and the rapid gyrations of my feet, I probably looked a bit like one of those "Gangnam" dancers on steroids. Fortunately, the ants hadn't been on me long enough to penetrate much of my clothing and I think they were probably too scared to bite. I finally settled down and finished brushing the remains off with my hands and looked around to see where they had come from. The front seat of the truck had an ancient wood-bead seat cover on it, covering a break in the stitching of the upholstery and the ants had built a nest inside the seat. There were millions of them and don't tell me I'm exaggerating; I didn't stop to count them! Would you? Well, to cut a long story short, I hurried down to the garden shed and found two spray-cans of Ant-killer and thoroughly doused the entire interior of the cab. The next day I went to inspect the driver's seat and there were just a few patches of, what looked like, black dust. Those ants must have been really scared!

Later on in the day I was putting some pine-cones into the burn-barrel and saw that there was a thriving ant colony in there too. There weren't enough pine-cones in there to justify a "burn" so they'll have to wait a little longer to get incinerated. I was just lucky they weren't "Fire ants," at least, not yet!

There doesn't seem to be much going on in the world of wildlife recently. Too hot and humid, is my guess. At least it is for me and my outside chores are suffering because of it. But it won't be long now before the cooler weather is here and my T-shirts will be the long sleeved kind. It's amusing, isn't it? In just a few weeks we'll be shivering and just wishing we could have

a day like today. One thing you can say about humans –

We're fairly easy to please but very hard to satisfy.

I HATE SPIDERS!

You would think that there must be some use for the spider, but I really can't think of one that would justify its existence. That is one creature that defies my love for all wild-life. I can't stand the things. Up until recently there existed a spider, hiding behind a down-spout at the corner of the house, who insisted on building a web, every night, between the corner of the house and the near-by Snow-ball tree. Every morning I would go out to the car and walk right into the web and have to spend quite a few minutes trying to brush the thing off my face with my hands. All the time hoping the neighbors couldn't hear me! Finally I remembered to do something about it and I purchased a spray can of Spider Killer. When I returned from the store, I took the spray can and let fly with the killer spray all up and down behind the down-spout. If the poison didn't kill him, the amount of liquid would have drowned him, I'm sure.

Having dealt with my main arachnoidal antagonist, I decided to go all around the house, spraying all spider webs. I followed up that operation with a broom attack to remove all evidence of my seemingly heartless attack on some of Mother Nature's creations. The following morning when it was still not full daylight, I went out the sun-room door to go feed the ducks and walked straight into a big, sticky spider web! Even the ducks must have been embarrassed at what they heard next and I do believe I saw two of the swans turn pink! It was just too much. After the blue smoke cleared and I had cleared most of the web from my glasses and my face, I got my almost empty spray can and soaked the eaves and door frame with all that was left in it. If I never see another spider anywhere, it will be too soon!

This incident reminded me of my worst ever encounter with the eight-legged little monsters. That was in Kenya, almost sixty years ago. I was a member of a Model Aircraft club which had the use of an acre of farm-land, for use as a flying field. The farmer was also a member. Anyway, on this particular day, the weather was very hot and of the two dozen or so club members there, about half had removed their shirts and were just wearing shorts and sneakers. I was one of them.

Our 1 acre patch which served as a take-off and landing area was situated about 300 yards from the edge of a wild and dense expanse of brush and forest. Some might call it a "jungle out there." On this particular day I would be test-flying a new model, 8ft wingspan, .65 cubic inch engine and single channel radio control. Now remember, that was in the very early days of remote control. The control system only allowed for the movement of one control surface. In this case, that was the rudder. The radio signal range was fairly limited, too and if I hadn't been so keen to see if my model would fly, I would have checked it out more thoroughly. Anyway, I cranked up the motor and the 'plane moved off across the field at a good speed, lifting off before it ran out of runway. It climbed away smoothly, gaining altitude and at about 200 feet I hit the rudder and turned it into the downwind leg of the first circuit. It responded perfectly until it went out of range. And then it was on its own, heading down-wind towards the woods. The standard response to that sort of thing was to take off running, with a friend, to try to keep up with the 'plane and to locate its landing site.

Running at full speed (those were the days!) into the elephant grass and mpani trees I was trying to keep the model in sight and was not looking where I was going. I burst through the elephant grass into what I thought was a relatively clear patch of widely spaced mpani trees and charged at full speed straight across it. I had only gone about half way to the other side when I felt sticky and itchy all over my chest and legs. I looked down and saw that I had run through several dozen spider webs, strung between the trees. These were really heavy duty webs and their owners were busy all over me stinging and biting. They were large black and yellow striped spiders and I guess they thought they had caught several big meals all in one go.

Anyway, to cut a long story short, after groggily driving myself home I swelled up like the Michelin Man and it was four days before I could go back to work. I really, really hate spiders!

FALLING LEAVES

Once again it's that time of year when that children's story hero might be declaring "The sky is falling!!" And once again I am annoyed at one of my neighbors who absolutely refuses to trim his hedge and trees which separate our properties. The hedge is at least twelve feet high in places and the oak, pine and sweet-gum trees hang low over my front yard, almost burying my old Dodge truck in leaves, pine straw, sweet gum balls and rotten tree limbs. He inherited the house from his Grand-parents who used to be my friends and they always kept the hedge neatly trimmed to the height of the chain-link fence that backs it. It seems he only uses the place at week-ends and I have yet to see him doing any yard work when he is there. And I'm getting too old to do my own yard work, never mind his!

Well, I'm sorry to be bending your ear but sometimes I just have to "sound off" to get my blood pressure under control, if you know what I mean. It helps but I can't fully express my feelings, the Editor would never publish it!

Wow! I feel better already.

Now back to the main business at hand. Sometimes, recently, I have been a little late serving breakfast to the duck population of Swan Lake and the wildlife let me know all about it. The racket they create is amazing. There are over one hundred ducks, a couple of dozen geese and a Swan Family of four, all pushing and shoving to get to the food first. And all except the Swans are really vocal in their complaints. I try to be there on time but I also have another task to perform on a couple of early mornings per week. The wild-life, however, do not accept that as an excuse. But I have found a way to quiet them down. Recently I have become a fan of the T.V. Program, "Duck Dynasty" and I purchased a "D.D." cap at Walmart. to wear at the Breakfast Club meetings at Miller's Store.

I had been to the Store one day last week and came home in time to give the ducks some food. I had forgotten that I was still wearing the hat and I went down to the shed and put some food in the bucket and took it down to the water. It was only just light enough for me to make out the birds but they could obviously see me! As soon as I arrived at the sea-wall, it seemed like the whole lake exploded in front of me! All the birds who can fly, took off together in such a rush of frantically flapping wings and feet that I was pretty well drenched with all the water they kicked up. The only ones left behind were the Swans and they just sat there, looking around in disbelief. I gave them some food and while they were eating, I removed the hat and the other birds who had settled down again, out in the middle of the lake, tentatively made their way back towards us. I think they were a little bit embarrassed by their behavior; they hardly made a sound. They all settled down to eat with only the occasional "quack".

Something else which has been causing disruptions of the Swan Lake Breakfast Club meetings recently has been the return of the Big Fish. The birds don't like sharing their food with the local denizens of the deep. In addition to some fairly big cat-fish there is a shoal of really big carp who occasionally raid the party and when they arrive they knock the birds away from the food with their tails. With open mouths they swim close to the surface, sucking down the food pellets as they go, like a team of underwater inverted vacuum cleaners. It doesn't take long for them to clean up and go on their way and I feel sorry for the birds and give them extra rations, to

make up for the intrusion.

A RAINY DAY

Saturday, the 14th of December and solid gray skies, drenching the lake and surrounding countryside with almost non-stop rain all morning, have silenced the wild-life. There is an eerie stillness in the air with no breeze to lighten the mood. It's depressing and it reminds me of living in England where this could well have been a typical summer's day. I know the old saying that "Into each life a little rain must fall" but just how much is a little? I've just checked the T.V. schedule and there isn't even any re-run episodes of my favorite show, "Duck Dynasty" on tonight to lighten my mood.

The past week was interesting though. Last Saturday morning I honored a promise previously made to a good friend of mine, Ray Miller, a member of the Miller's Store Breakfast Club. He had asked me if I would speak to a group of Men's Club members at the Union Church on Hwy 155. They were particularly interested in how World War II had affected children in England at that time. Now that was the first time I had ever stood up and addressed a group of people and I must admit, I felt somewhat nervous at first but it didn't take too long for me to warm up to it. I couldn't really explain what the war meant to most kids in England because I lived mainly in a farming area where there was nothing for the enemy to bomb. If anything, I would say, the war taught a lot of us kids to be independent. If we wanted anything we had to find it, make it, or do without it. And that is brought home to me, especially at this time of the year when the shops are full of this year's latest and greatest "gifts". Our greatest "gifts" were life and each other. We did manage to get into a fair amount of mischief, with which to amuse ourselves, and some of that is detailed in my books, "Bumps in the Road, Part One" and "More Bumps in the Road, Part Two". Both of these are in your local library along with a collection of my columns, titled "Reflections on Swan Lake" written for The Henry County Times. They make excellent Christmas presents and are available from any good bookseller, on order, and on line from Amazon.com

The other big event in my life, during the past week was last Thursday evening. Millie and I attended the Miller's Mill Breakfast Club Christmas Party held at the Union Church. There were over eighty people present and I found it interesting trying to identify the members when they were all in their "Going to meeting" gear and without their ball-caps. It's amazing what a difference a cap can make to anyone's appearance.

The food of course was outstanding and both Millie and I ate more than we should have done. We couldn't miss Herman's biscuits on Friday morning but I did miss lunch. I was still full. Before we ate, Herman led and conducted the carol singing and Ray performed his Master of Ceremony duties with his usual polish and aplomb. Overall it was an outstanding evening spent with old and new friends and I know I will never forget it. The organization and effort put into the event by the ladies in the kitchen and the young people who helped everything run smoothly was really appreciated.

But then it was time to leave and as we had left out two kids "home alone" I was anxious to get back to them. They were fine, of course, and greeted us with high excitement as if we had been gone for two weeks, instead of just a couple of hours. I had to withstand the "sulks" from Sammy that go along with any absence of mine. That lasts for the following day, just to teach me a lesson, and then he gets over it. After that we are "Best Buddies" again.

Tonight is Millie's Sunday School Class Christmas Party and I know she is looking forward to that. I'll be staying home with the kids so they won't feel too bad. I just can't go off and leave them for another evening, so soon after the last one. They really are high up on my list of blessings.

Well, if this does get printed before Christmas, I would like to wish all readers of the Times, a wonderful, safe and merry Christmas. And if it doesn't, I hope y'all had a great time and remembered the reason for the season!

MORE MUSCOVYS

It was a very cold dawn this morning when I went down to the water to feed the ducks. My outside thermometer read 23 degrees. I was wearing two shirts, a sweater and a heavy jacket and after about five minutes out there, I could hardly feel my feet or my fingers. I just can't tolerate extremes of temperature any more. Anyway, when I had finished feeding all the birds and the squirrels, I came indoors to thaw out. Dee hadn't even got out of bed so Sammy cuddled up alongside me in the old recliner. We stayed there for a couple of hours, watching the political discussions on the news which I find quite entertaining as long as I don't take all the lies seriously. If I did, I'm sure that my blood pressure would go through the roof and my fibrillating old ticker would probably explode.

Anyway, I had thawed out nicely, thanks to my "Duck Dynasty" throw-rug and a warm-bodied Sammy so, as the sun was shining brightly by then, with no wind to speak of, I decided to go into the back yard again to do a little yard work. Not too much, because it still felt chilly to me. "Pine-cone picking", I started out with my 5 gallon pail and my "grabber" and went into Barry's yard first but there weren't many there. I picked up the few that had fallen since Monday and came back into my yard. Again, there weren't enough there to really make it worthwhile, but I picked them up with a few small pine tree limbs which had come down with loads of pine straw. I dumped them all in my old burn-barrel.

I was standing with my back to the water, looking at all the pinestraw laying on the concrete picnic area when I sensed a movement behind me. I eased around slowly, not wanting to scare away whatever it was, and close up to the sea wall there were four beautiful

Muscovy ducks. Of course, I couldn't help talking to

them. I asked them if they would like some breakfast and

they assured me that they would. By the time I had gone

to the shed and come back with a scoop of duck food,

they had been joined by another six! So now we have ten

beautifully colored ducks, no two alike, to feed and

enjoy. Just when I was feeling a little down these

wonderful creatures appeared. That was a true spirit-lifter

for me.

SWAN LAKE ICE AGE

Today is the 11th January, 2014 and four mornings ago, on the 7th, the temperature when I was feeding the ducks was 5 F. That "F" really does stand for Fahrenheit! This morning it was 57 F. Go figure! The ice has all melted and if it wasn't for the siphon system in the dam, we would have been flooded out if you count in the amount of rain we are experiencing this morning. Just what is going on with the weather? Is someone trying to draw our attention to the fact that all is not going well with the world and that we, humanity that is, need to make some serious changes in our behavior patterns? I've made some changes in my life recently, late though that may be. I just hope it isn't too late.

Well, let's change the subject there and get back to the wild life here at Swan Lake. I told you about the sudden influx of Muscovy ducks to the feathered population and how attractive they are. They still have a few red lumps on their heads but that doesn't detract from their beautiful plumage. One morning last week I was walking along the wooden fence by the waterfront when this large, dark-colored bird came swooping in over the lake straight towards me. No more than four feet away from me, it landed precariously on the top stringer of the fence and sat there, wobbling, trying to maintain its balance. It made me think of a D.U.I. suspect failing a road-side sobriety test. The gyrations soon subsided and I could see that it was one of the Muscovys, with almost black feathers which glowed a metallic green color when the sun shone on them. We stood and stared at each other for a few seconds before it spread it's wings and flew off. "Thanks for dropping in!" I called, as it headed for the opposite shore.

Last week, when on a grocery buying trip to my favorite grocery store, Ingles, I noticed some 1lb clear plastic containers of Christmas nuts on sale. I knew my back-yard squirrels would enjoy them so I bought one and each morning, when I fill the bird-feeder I put half a dozen or so in the small wire baskets at the ends of the feeder. That supplements their Christmas present, a large pressed corn block suspended on a spring hanger from one end of the bird feeder. The birds and the squirrels seem to share their "goodies" quite happily and looking out of the window a few moments ago I watched as two squirrels and three doves waded into the large puddle of rain-water at the base of the feeder pole hunting seeds and nuts which had fallen from the feeder above. Two totally different species, coexisting happily. And we're supposed to be the smart ones?

Today, being Saturday, Millie was in charge of the

Kids' usual morning outing which normally consists of a fast-food breakfast in the car and then a quick tour of any yard sales she can find. Hey, everyone should have a hobby, right? Her's is yard sales, mine is writing to you! Anyway, I decided to visit "Biscuits and Brunch", Johny Bassler's place on Burke Street in Stockbridge. By the number of customer's there it must be a very popular place for breakfast and I saw two more Miller's Store Breakfast Club members sitting at a table for three, so I joined them. The rain outside was torrential at the time but no-one seemed to notice. Nothing could dilute the cozy, friendly, family atmosphere inside which made breakfast a very, enjoyable and tasty event. I could be having breakfast there on several Saturday mornings in future.

On a more somber note, I have to report the death of one of the Muscovys. This one was mostly white and I first saw him laying in the weeds at the side of the road by the swampy area of the lake. He was just a bundle of white feathers with two feet sticking up in the air. Another, mainly white, Muscovy sat a few feet away from him. I said earlier that I had made some changes in my life, one of which was not to judge others when I didn't know the whole story but it certainly grieves me that such a beautiful, innocent creature should die just because someone was in a hurry for whatever reason. The speed limit there is only 25 m.p.h.

THE MIGHTY SWEET GUM BITES THE DUST!

The day finally arrived when my neighbor who owns the small forest adjoining the southern boundary of my property, decided that one part of it which had been causing me much aggravation, should be removed. He actually came and told me that he had made arrangements to have the sweet gum and the nearby huge bushy Magnolia tree removed. I asked him what he intended to do about the overgrown hedge between our properties but he just turned his back and walked away. A week later, a man knocked on my door and introduced himself as the owner of the company who had been assigned the job of taking down and removing the two offending trees. He asked if he could use my driveway and part of my front lawn on which to drop the tree parts as they came down. I instantly agreed, providing no damage was done to my property and at 11 a.m. the following day, a small fleet of heavy equipment arrived. The sweet gum was the most difficult being almost 100 feet tall and hanging over two power lines alongside the road. At least, it looked difficult to me but that team of experts made short work of the entire job and had everything cut down, cleaned up and hauled away within two hours. Just for reference, the company's name is Pro Tree Service of Jonesborough and I was very impressed with their work.

So that was the end of two of the causes of so much tree debris and leaves in my front yard. There are about a dozen more, smaller, trees that need the same treatment but I suppose I have to be thankful for having partial relief. The hedge still remains a major source of inconvenience and I spent two days, last week, attacking it from my side of the fence with loppers, shears and a shovel. I still have at least another couple of days work there; I can only push myself for a couple of hours at a time. Having a "trick" ticker, I wear out much quicker these days and it has taken most of a week to recover from that unaccustomed exercise.

I know I have been talking a lot about Muscovy ducks lately but I can't help telling you about the latest trick they have been playing on me. I normally take the Kids for their car ride between 8.30 and 9.30 a.m. A couple of days ago, when we went outside to the car, three of the Muscovites, family name "The Uglies", were strolling around on the front lawn. The Kids and I went for the usual 50 yard walk up the road and back to allow for any urgent relief stops before getting into the car and I left them there for a couple of minutes while I went to the shed to get a scoop of duck food. I didn't like the

"Uglies" wandering around so close to the road and when I showed them the scoop in my hand and walked back down to the water, they followed and jumped back into the lake to get a breakfast snack without being bothered by swans, common ducks and geese. Of course, by the time we reached the water, four other family members had caught on to what was happening and they all joined in. Naturally that meant another trip to the shed to get a second scoop of food for the newcomers. Is it any wonder that I stay so poor? Anyway, every morning since then the same scenario has been played out in the front yard. They know what they want and have quickly learned how to get it. They really are much smarter than we give them credit for.

ICY MIX-UP, JANUARY 2014

What a mess! And the only ones who seemed to be able to cope with the situation were the wild-life. The ducks and the geese took it all in their stride and even the swans were seen navigating the ice floes on the lake with very little difficulty. They did have to try harder and probably lost a little "face" when they had to struggle to get back onto the ice after dropping back into the water when they got too close to the edge. Overall size and weight can be a definite disadvantage in those circumstances. The other denizens of the lake refrained from commenting on the display, realizing no doubt, that if they did, they would have to pay for it dearly when the situation returned to normal. In any event, no waterfowl were abandoned on the side of the lake and no collisions were reported. No young birds were left behind to spend the night in strange and uncomfortable surroundings and the entire flock managed to survive the night without the aid of any "authorities."

After breakfast was served at daylight, they all slowly, if not elegantly, waddled away across the ice in search of more sustenance at other locations around the lake. As they moved out into the gloom of early morning, I gave them a couple of "Good-Byes" on my duck call to which they replied cheerfully, as they disappeared into the pre-dawn mists.

I couldn't help thinking about all the unfortunate human beings out there with all their technology to help them, trapped by the snow and ice, unable to move or get to where they needed to be. Could we be doing wrong; not living life the way we are supposed to? Could this be part of our punishment? The whole incident certainly gave me some soul-searching moments and I have promised myself and the Creator that I really will try harder in future.

And then there was the Super Bowl. I really can't comment too much on that as I am not a foot-ball fan but from the little I saw of it, I'd say that someone does a better job of selling pizzas than he does throwing a ball. That game reminded me of a time, almost thirty years ago, when I first came to the U.S.A. and became interested in professional wrestling. I was naive enough to believe that it was all "real." I've learned a lot since then, believe me!

Yesterday wasn't entirely wasted as far as I was concerned. I had been given a gift card at Christmas so Millie, the Kids and I piled into Millie's Toyota and we set off to go to Caraba's for a take-out meal, after calling the order in. The kerb-service was right on time and we were soon home enjoying(?) a restaurant meal in comfort with our family. Based on my resolution to be less critical in my judgments in future I will just refer to the meal as adequate but hardly worth the price. Anyway, it didn't take too long and we soon got back to watching Puppy-Bowl on T.V., a big improvement over the so-called Super Bowl. I fully understand that all the "plays" were set-ups but the producers and directors made them seem just as real as the full-size version and, to my mind, much more enjoyable.

So, here we are again with the sun shining and the temperature in the low sixties, no wind to speak of and all the ice and snow, things of the past. It certainly is a crazy, mixed up season and I can't help wondering if humanity, as a whole, would just try to "straighten up and fly right" maybe we could get back to regular seasons of Winter, Spring, Summer and Fall.

EARLY SPRING FEVER

Still recovering from that excess of exercise after the demise of the sweet gum tree, I haven't been able to get a whole lot done in the yard recently. The weather has looked to be cooperating until I ventured outside and then the wind picked up and the icy grip of Winter rapidly reminded me that I was not as young as I used to be. It doesn't seem to bother the water-fowl, though. How they can all sit and splash around in that cold water at day-break is beyond my comprehension. I never have been a fan of cold weather. One of the reasons I've never been keen on returning to England for any length of time, is the climate. I know that may sound silly but I really mean it when I say that if I never see another snow-flake it will be too soon and the only ice I would welcome would be in a glass of sweet tea or some other form of adult beverage. I don't expect to be seeing much of the up-coming Winter Olympics either, but each to his own.

Thinking about "sporting events", the annual megafuss has been warming up for a few weeks now and will soon occupy all the news channels with endless re-runs and analyses. I'm thinking of the Super Bowl, of course. I'll be watching Puppy Bowl X on Animal Planet. I think that will be much better entertainment, for me anyhow. But as I just said, "Each to his own."

I hope I'm not "Jumping the gun" but yesterday, I believe I saw an early sign of Spring. Or maybe it was just wishful thinking. Anyway, the sun was shining brightly and I couldn't resist going through the sun-room out onto the top of the steps into the back yard, just to see if the weather was as warm and pleasant as it looked. Of course I was disappointed, although the wind wasn't blowing so it was still a "nice" day. I looked out across the lake, admiring the view, when I caught a glimpse of a blue flash out of the corner of my eye. I looked around and the closest cover was the arbor, overgrown with bare honey-suckle vines which did little to hide a brilliant blue-bird, the first I have seen this year. I then noticed several small birds in the jungle of vines and a somewhat muted chorus of birdsong filtered through the branches. It sounded as if the feathered choristers were not quite sure if their timing was right. I suppose we will have to wait and see what the ground-hog has to say next week.

Well, it's about time for the Kids to have their morning ride in the car, up to Ingles store in the village. They are not the only creatures who know how to tell time around here. When we go outside I can just about guarantee that at least one Muscovy duck will be waiting for us to leave the house. By the time we've gone to "empty the tanks" before getting in the car, the rest of the flock will have joined him. This has become a daily routine and they know that I will put the Kids in the car while I go down to the shed to get them a scoop, or two, of food pellets. This all started one day when I carried a scoop of food to the gray Muscovy who was scavenging around the base of the bird feeder. We had a short meeting and parted on the best of terms but he must have gone back to the rest of the family and told them that I was an easy mark for a free meal. I guess he was right but I really do it to get them away from the road and back into the water. I would hate to be responsible for the loss of another beautiful Swan Lake resident.

IT'S GONE!

It's so good to see the ducks paddling around instead of ice-skating across the lake and to be able to walk down to the mail-box without slipping and sliding, risking life or limb, to see if there were any advertisements in there that I hadn't seen a dozen times before. Anyway, for a while at least, snow and ice are things of the past and we now have a great Spring to anticipate.

Thinking of Spring, I was picking up pine cones and other pine tree related debris from my neighbor's yard and my own, after the snow had melted and I noticed that the daffodil bulbs had sprouted leaves about three inches high and I'm sure they weren't above the surface before the snow. Maybe they needed the blanket of snow to warm them while we were experiencing below freezing temps. Well, to me it was a good sign.

Yesterday I was doing a little yard work, clearing dead and dying vegetation and burning it up in my old burn-barrel when I was "accosted" by four hungry Muscovy ducks. I just can't look a hungry duck in the beak when both he and I know that there is food available in the shed. They have now become bold enough to fly over my fence and land in the weed patch, laughingly referred to as my lawn and I can expect a visit at any time when I am outside. Anyway, I put my shovel down and went towards the shed with the "Gang" following. While I was inside, getting the food, they stood quietly together, making no attempt to follow me inside the shed. When I came out with the food bucket in my hand they showed their appreciation with a rapid waving about of their rapidly opening and closing beaks and it looked as though they had already started eating the food, in their imaginations. I decided to make them wait a little while

longer and headed for the dock. It probably looked like I

was being kidnapped by the Gang as they followed close

behind. When we arrived at the dock, I turned to face my

"captors" and sat on a couple of concrete blocks. I dipped

my hand into the bucket and pulled out a handful of food

pellets and offered it to them. I guess they thought I was

trying to catch them and they backed away from my

hand, just out of reach. I tried dropping a few on the dock

planks, just in front of them and they quickly gobbled

them up. I then tried dropping some more just an inch or

two closer to me and eventually had them literally eating

out of my hand. I did get a couple of nips for my trouble

when all four of them tried to snatch food from my

fingers at the same time but it was worth it to have won

their trust. It's nice to have company when I'm working in

the yard, even if I don't get a whole lot done when they're

hanging around being "cute". Even Sammy and Dee seem to have granted them visiting rights and just ignore them as if they belong there. Fortunately the swans don't seem to be troubling them too much and I can't help feeling that the Muscovies may have got the message across to them that they are also Swan Lake residents and they have rights, too. When they had eaten enough they waddled over to the edge of the dock and hopped back into the water while I stood up and walked over to another part of the yard where there were a couple of large weeds that needed to be pulled.

The next morning, just before daybreak, I walked down to the shed to get the duck-food for the usual breakfast. Swans, ducks and geese were all gathered, waiting impatiently for me to bring out the food bucket but I couldn't find it! The air was starting to turn blue, either from the approaching dawn or my language, when

I remembered leaving it on the dock the previous day. After collecting it, it was still too dark to see properly when I returned to the shed for the food but the hand holding the bucket handle started itching and stinging a little. I turned on a small work light in the shed and saw that my hand and arm was covered in little black ants who didn't appreciate having their early morning meal disturbed. Once again I performed my version of some kind of pop dance while furiously beating myself all over to get rid of those little flesh-eating parasites. I hope nobody saw me!

Anyway, to cut a long story short, the whole thing cost me my favorite jacket because the zipper toggle came off in the wash and it would cost more to replace the zipper than the coat originally cost. Maybe that will teach me not to be so forgetful. And how long will it take for me to forget that I said that?

COOTS & COMPANY

I told you, some time ago, that a new type of duck had taken up residence at Swan Lake but I didn't know its name. Well, now I know. My neighbor, Barry, told me that the little black ducks with white beaks are known as Coots. They were very shy, at first, but they are becoming more and more bold each day. Their numbers seem to be increasing as well, but I haven't seen any babies. Maybe the original "settlers" are sending out "c-mails" on the duck network, telling friends and relatives that they have found a great place to live where the climate isn't too bad and they get free snacks! The only other "Coots" that I've heard of are the "Old" variety, of which I am one.

I just looked out the window and saw a rather

unusual sight. Two very large white birds were skimming the water, side by side. It was the young couple, offspring of Big Daddy, trying out their flying prowess while they are still able to. They haven't had their wings clipped yet and, quite honestly, I hope they never do. They should be free to fly as their Creator intended and if they could take their grand-parents with them I, for one, wouldn't lose any sleep over that. And I'm pretty sure the Canada geese would agree with me there! The swans are beautiful to watch as they cruise around the lake but they are total bullies when it comes to their neighbors. Could there be a Russian connection there? Maybe I should leave that one alone, for now! I'll stick with the local Muscovies and leave the Muscovites in peace.

The friendly Muscovies around here get tamer every day. Now that they know where the food is kept and recognize the one who feeds them, I have that pleasure at least once a day. The youngest are the most tame and have no problem eating out of my hand but the older, larger birds hang back waiting for food to be thrown on the ground for them. I'm sure they will come around eventually and I'll keep trying. Yesterday I was feeding them on the dock at the bottom of my yard. Two small ones and two large. An adult Canada goose also decided to join the party and he came very close to taking a chance on pecking some food out of my hand but he just couldn't quite make it. Hopefully he will have watched the others eating out of my hand and next time he might have gained a little more confidence. A pair of fishermen, in a john-boat, watched us for a while. When one of the ducks decided she had eaten enough and flew over to a corner of the cove, about thirty yards away, the fishermen also moved over in that direction. I was watching the boat as it moved away and then suddenly noticed, what looked like a struggle, going on in the water just beyond the boat. Thinking that the duck may have got into trouble, I called out to the fishermen, "Hey, has that duck over there got a problem of some kind?" "Not yet," came the reply. "The one on the bottom will probably have one, in the near future but they're not fighting, they're mating."

That reminds me. Yesterday, my neighbor, Barry, called out to me when I was in the back yard. He was playing basketball with one of his grandsons. "Hey, Don, can you come over here when you're finished?" "Sure, I'll be right there." I replied. I put the feed bucket back in the shed and made my way over to Barry's yard, hoping that he wasn't going to try to get me to play ball. I'm much too old for that s.....tuff, as the man said in the movie. Anyway, when I arrived Barry told me to look behind the bush just outside his garage, up beside the house. There was a bowl-shaped nest scooped out in the dirt containing seven plain white eggs. We were all excited about the event and proud to think that the bird had been comfortable enough with us to trust us with her future family. I believe it was the mostly gray colored Muscovy that I had just finished feeding, down by the dock, when he called me. The next time it is a sunny day, I'll go back there and take some pictures.

DAISY, THE DUCK WITH A BUTLER!

The latest news from the Duck World, at Swan Lake, is the anticipated arrival of baby Muscovy ducks to add to the flock. Daisy, (now that she's going to be a Momma, she has to have a name) started off with a nest between a bush and the back wall of my neighbor's house. Not a really fancy nest, just an indentation in the mulch and dirt, big enough to hold four eggs. Every night she added a couple more eggs to the collection. After she had laid over twenty eggs she settled in to nurse them by spreading herself out over the eggs after covering them with dry leaves and down, plucked from her body. That makes a comfortable, warm blanket for the brood.

And now all we have to do is wait for the arrival of her new family. In the mean time though, I hadn't seen Daisy move from the nest to get food or water for herself.

After a couple of days, after giving breakfast to the other birds in the lake, I took two small plastic bowls over to Daisy, one with the usual food I give to the ducks and one for water. I offered her some of the food in my hand and she eagerly took some. I tried to get her to drink some water but she wasn't interested so I put both the water and food bowls on the ground within easy reach for her. She seemed quite content with what I had done for her so I repeated the performance the next day and every day since. With Barry and his two boys keeping a watch over them during the day and me providing sustenance for the mother-to-be in the mornings, we are all hoping for a successful hatching, sometime this month.

So that's the story of how I became a Butler to a duck!

Changing the subject completely, several months ago, I had a terrible noise coming from the front of my ancient Chevy Lumina and I took it to the Lorraine Community Garage on Union Church Road. My old friend, Durant Godwin a.k.a. Auto Doc, had recommended them to me before he passed away last May. Tom Turner, the owner, found that the a/c compressor was "shot" and, as I couldn't afford a new one at that time, he rigged a pulley to take its place. In the winter, it was cold enough not to need an a/c and the Kids were quite happy. It's more their car than mine anyway. Of course, as soon as the weather started to warm up, both Sammy and Dee let me know that it was now time to get the a/c operating again and last week I took it back to Tom and he replaced the pulley with another compressor. I have to admit that the Kids were right. It's much more comfortable with the a/c functioning properly and I can see the old car lasting us through the "Quarter million miles target" which I had set for her. Only six thousand more to go!

Now that Spring seems to have finally arrived I am hoping to see some more baby ducks and geese on the lake. It has been ages since I last saw any geese or duck families on parade. But it is good to see the humming birds are back. My old friend, the Redneck hummer just paid a visit to my feeder a few moments ago. I think it was he who hovered outside my window on the evening of April 1st, giving me the reminder to get the feeder out and ready to operate.

Yesterday I started the annual chain of yard related chores by "bush hoggin' the weed patch" in the back yard. That means getting out my trusty old Snapper, which started on the third pull and with the cut set at the highest it would go, I knocked the weeds down to a level where wild animals can no longer hide from view. I still have a way to go before the place is presentable but as long as the weather cooperates it shouldn't take more than a couple of months. What used to take me a few hours can consume several days. The hardest part is just getting started. I find that these days my "get up and go" has mostly "got up and gone." 'Til next time...........

DUCK DEPOT

With apologies to A&E and the Robertson family, this is the poor man's version of a certain well-known and loved television show. I'm just kidding; it's just that life recently has seemed somewhat like a reality show, with so much going on in an otherwise very peaceful existence, here on Swan Lake.

My very good friend and next-door neighbor, Barry, and his family went away for the Easter weekend. It was Saturday morning when a burglar invaded his house and stole a load of Barry's possessions. Supposedly this happened around 6.30 a.m., just about the time when I was feeding the ducks and providing food and water for the Muscovy duck, sitting on eggs in her nest beside the garage. The only thing I noticed which was out of the ordinary was the open door to the garage, which I closed thinking that maybe one of the kids had left it open. An hour or so later, the police were on the scene and I gave my statement as to what I had seen and what I knew about the incident, which was very little.

All the excitement and "hubbub" must have stirred Daisy, the Momma duck, to try harder and a couple of days later, Barry, who had returned in a hurry from his Easter trip, knocked on my front door and told me to rush over to his yard. I thought, maybe, that something was wrong with the Muscovy momma. I put on my yard shoes and dashed over to the nest site and immediately saw two little yellow bundles of fur groggily trying to get back under Momma's skirts. There was another one lying still, not too far away, who had obviously not made the transition from a comfortable and safe harbor in the shell to the somewhat harsh reality of the world.

So that was the start of the "hatching" with three down and about twenty-one to go. This is the first time I have ever been this closely concerned with the duck breeding process and I've learned quite a bit. I also remembered the old saying "Don't count your chickens before they've hatched," and found that it applies equally as well, to ducks. The final count was eight ducklings including the one dead one. After that Daisy showed no interest in sitting on the remaining sixteen eggs and started off leading the seven babies on a walking tour of Barry's back yard.

In the mean time, I was busy cleaning up an old pet carrier which I had in the crawl space under the house and I set it up alongside the nest site with food and water dishes, thinking that the family might take up residence there. But it was not to be. I was in the middle of rigging a form of ramp for them to get down into the lake. It was a drop of about eighteen inches and I thought it would be too high for the little ones to jump in and then have no way to get out. One of them fell in while I was working on it and I fished him out with my old dip-net. I guess that must have been some kind of signal to Daisy because the next time I turned round I saw her leading her little troup across the yard and out onto Barry's dock. One baby disappeared over the edge, followed by Daisy and then the rest of the babies piled in, in a big splash.

For a moment I considered diving in after them and then I realized that they probably knew what they were doing better than I did. So I just shaded the sun from my eyes with my hand and watched them as they formed up behind their momma and paddled away towards the North end of the lake. I thought that after all I had done for them, they might have looked back as they went or at least thrown me a wing-wave of farewell, but "out of sight, out of mind" I guess. I just hope and pray that none of the predators, like turtles, blue cranes, catfish and snakes might get them. Maybe Daisy will come back to visit one day but I doubt if I'll recognize the babies. Ah well, that's life, I guess.

I did manage to get a couple of photographs of them before they left and I showed them around at the Breakfast Club meeting the following morning. I told the members that I was suffering from the "Empty nest syndrome." Not a lot of sympathy there, I'm afraid, among country folk. They'd seen it all before. Hey, I've been called an idiot many times before and I'm sure I will be again!

THE TURTLE TROT

Once again Mother Nature reminded me that I'm not getting any younger and, what used to be nothing more than an easy jog is now a fairly major undertaking, involving numerous aches and pains in my lower extremities. Returning from a trip to my favorite grocery store, Ingles, one day last week, I was approaching Swan Lake on Knollwood drive. As I crested the rise on my way down to meet up with Lakeshore Drive, I spotted a large lump in the middle of the road. There was no other traffic on the road at that time and I slowed down and stopped the car just a couple of feet from a fair sized turtle. I just knew that someone else, in a hurry, might come down the hill and ruin that little fellow's whole day.

I left the car door open as I got out and bent over to pick up the wanderer but he really didn't fancy being picked up by a stranger or perhaps "he" was a "she" and was just playing shy. Anyway, with a quick rattle of claws on the blacktop, "it" did a quick circle and started back up the hill, staying in the middle of the road leaving me, bent over like the Hunchback of Notre Dame staggering along trying to catch up. And "it" was pulling away from me! This wasn't working the way I had planned so I stopped and straightened up and walked slowly in its direction. When I got to within a couple of steps, it suddenly raced towards me, dodged around my ankles before I could bend down to grab it and headed back down the hill. I swung round and watched as it raced away from me and just before it reached the bottom of the slope, it peeled off to the right and disappeared in the grass and weeds at the road-side. I wasn't too happy at the thought that a little turtle could out-pace me but at least it had another chance at life which, I guess, was important to both of us.

I haven't seen any more of the little family of Muscovy Ducks that I tried to help, although the mother, Daisy, did stop by one day when I was in the back yard, to get a quick snack. I gave her a handful of Ingles dog food pellets, which they all seem to enjoy. She didn't stay very long and I had the feeling that she was more than a little ashamed that she didn't have any babies with her and that she was relieved that I hadn't asked any embarrassing questions. Once again, Mother Nature's plans for the ducklings must have been different from our's.

The only other babies I've seen on the lake this year were a trio of baby Canadas which I noted down by the swampy area, close to Lakeshore Drive. The parents were herding them back from the road towards the water and they had probably been teaching the young ones that being on the water is a whole lot safer for young geese than being on the road.

Normally we don't see many black crows at this time of the year but there is just one that seems to have decided that my yard is a good spot for a quick and easy meal of dog food. He suddenly appears on top of my garden shed examining the ground around the shed door, looking for spilled "Kibbles". Now that I know what he is searching for I always make sure to drop a few for him when I get the food for the ducks in the morning. Seeing that "commercial" on T.V. showing one candidate's opinion of the Washington scene as a bunch of babies, I was reminded of the mega meetings conducted in the high pines around the lake in the Spring by a large flock of crows. They seem to get a lot discussed and settled in a relatively short period of time and I'm sure the candidates could learn a lot from our feathered friends, if

they would just pay attention!

NORTHERN HENRY COUNTY "THINK TANK."

Today, being Friday, was my day to visit the Miller's Store Breakfast Club. Actually I also visit the Club on both Fridays and Mondays. There is only just so much fun that this tired, old ex-Brit can stand and the Store is just the place for me to get my allowance! Take this morning, for instance. I arrived a few minutes later than normal, at 5.15 a.m., and coffee had already been made. Mr. Miller the proprietor, and three other members had already started the day's discussions, touching lightly on weather, politics and the health of various other members. These and many other subjects would be examined more thoroughly when the rest of the membership arrived.

I poured myself a cup of the best coffee in Henry County and sat in my customary seat in one corner of the assembly. One of the oldest members was tracing part of the family tree of one of the oldest families in Henry County, and concluded that he was his own cousin! He decided that he would have to give this subject a closer look when the opportunity might present itself.

It wasn't long before more and more members arrived and the meeting room was full with some standing room on the sides. Everybody had views on one or more of the many subjects being scrutinized and the sound level rose in pitch as those of us who might be getting a "little hard of hearing" struggled to hear and understand the chatter. One member, a retired dentist, told a story about his attempt at farming after he retired from dentistry. He wanted to be a turkey farmer but he went broke after just a couple of weeks. He said that an agricultural agent had told him that he had planted his turkeys too deep and too close together! I know, it took me a few seconds to get it, too.

Listening in to several different conversations at the same time, I tried to concentrate on just one subject but it was impossible. Everything was just so interesting. One member was trying to teach a younger man how he was able to make a very precise engine part on a lathe while another was discussing the results of a cancer screening test that he had recently undergone. Yet another was describing his attempts to build a vegetable garden, while another reported on the welfare of his rescue dogs, and so it went on for almost two hours. And these were only a miniscule sample of the many and varied topics of conversation which continued almost non-stop.

It was obvious to any observer that this is a close group of friends who think highly of each other and who would do anything in their power to help out any member in need. There is even a clip-board containing "Get well" and "Best wishes" cards which is handed around for everyone present to sign. These cards are sent to any person needing a spiritual lift, in hospital or recuperating at home, known to any member.

So this is how I and about two dozen other senior "gentlemen" spend our early mornings at the Miller's Mill Store on Hwy 155. There are other groups who also frequent the store later in the day but the most active have to be the early risers. I had never realized that such a fine group of men with so many different backgrounds and interests could mix in so well. This is the first time I have been part of a Breakfast Club and I didn't even realize that such an organization existed. But I have since found out that there are others in other parts of the country which perform a similar function.

The Club makes collections throughout the year to

help people in the community who may have fallen on hard times and Mr. Miller's bicycle excursions to the coal-mining districts of Virginia are an annual event. I don't mean Herman rides a bicycle to Virginia but during the year he collects used bicycles from all different sources, fixes them up when they need attention and then, around Christmas time, the Breakfast Club helps him load up his truck and trailer. He delivers the bikes to needy people and children in the poorer regions of Virginia where work on the coal mines is declining. Last year he had received bicycle donations of more than thirty units. So if you have a bicycle that you would like to donate to a worthy cause, drop it off at the Miller's Store on Hwy 155 where it will be most welcome. And if you come early enough you might get a cup of the best coffee in the County!

IT LOOKS AND FEELS LIKE SUMMER

The weather appears to have settled down into a Summer-like pattern, at least according to the weather-men on T.V. But what they don't say is that it is a Central Florida-like pattern, not a Northern Georgia one. I remember being in central Florida one Summer when it was hot and humid every day with guaranteed thunderstorms every afternoon. In Northern Georgia at that time it was just hot and humid. Ah well, global warming is starting to make itself felt everywhere. We certainly can't complain when we look at the weather in the rest of the country. So far we are truly blessed.

And now to some news of wild life activities on the Lake. Recently I have had some small health issues which prevented me from serving breakfast on time (dawn) to the resident waterfowl on a couple of occasions. They couldn't understand why their morning snack should not be available at the usual first glimpse of daylight so three of them, namely the Muscovy Gang, made it their business to march up my garden path and camp out at the bottom of my sun-room steps. While two of them stayed on guard at the bottom of the steps, one of the two females waddled her way up to the top and peered in through the glass doors at me. I couldn't help thinking that they took all this trouble just because they were concerned about me but of course, it was really their snack that they were concerned about. Anyway, they had made their point so I just had to go down to the shed and get their treats for them.

The same routine took place the second time I couldn't make it early enough for them. And that time the lead female followed me into the shed to make sure, I suppose, that I wasn't short-changing them. But they really are some very friendly creatures and even though they don't appreciate being stroked, like a dog, they will readily eat out of my hand without tearing loose any of my fingers.

Well, I got over my "episodes" as I called them and am now back to my usual self. The extended family gets fed at dawn and all is well with the world! But just as I think that I am getting to understand the wild life a little better, they surprise me yet again. Now we have a pair of Mallard ducks that seem to think my back yard and particularly the area around the base of the bird feeder is their property. I've seen them chase other Mallards away and even put a couple of squirrels to flight. One thing is for sure, even without any other humans here during the day, I'm never lonely. Sammy and Dee aren't much company during the day. Neither of them enjoy the heat and apart from our usual daily, early morning excursion to Ingles store for grocery shopping and sometimes breakfast with a friend, they spend the rest of their day in the bedroom which is the coolest room in the house, catching up with their snoozing time.

Now I'd like to draw your attention to an event to be held on the McDonough square on June 14, that's next Saturday, from 1 to 4 p.m.   This is sponsored by the McDonough Arts Council and will provide a great opportunity for local authors to meet their readers and vice versa. Books will be available to purchase. I know I am really looking forward to this, hoping to meet some of my readers of this column and also some of those who may have already read my books. I have three previously published and another "in the works."

Well, that's about the end of my allowed space, for now, so I'll just sign off, hoping to see you on the Square, next Saturday between 1 and 4 p.m.

IT'S ALL I EVER WANTED!

One good thing about these pop-up showers in the afternoons is that everyone knows that it isn't a good thing for the mower to cut grass when it is soaking wet. And my grass has been soaked almost all and every day, recently. Except, maybe, for an hour or so around mid-day when it has dried up a little and then it is too hot for this old man to be out pushing or even guiding a mower. That's my excuse anyway, and I'm sticking to it!

Even the ducks have had to take shelter when some of these short-lived but very active showers take place. I've seen monsoon rains in Africa that have been more gentle than some of these "down-pours." I think "Toad-stranglers" is the technical term. Trying to see across the lake during one of these torrents is like trying to see through a solid cement wall and I couldn't help wondering how the siphon system in the dam is holding up. I finally got a chance to drive across the dam a couple of days ago. The road had been closed for months but I guess the 'powers that be' figured that everything that needed to settle had done so by now and had opened up the road to limited traffic.

It felt quite strange, like "deja vu", as though I was seeing my house and boat on the opposite shore for the first time. My imagination took me back twenty years to when I first saw the house when the realtor drove me across the dam in 1994 and pointed it out to me. She said, "That's the little house I was talking about," as she stopped the car and indicated the little gray siding house, next door to a large, brick-built residence which made its neighbor look very small. At first I thought she was talking about the big house but she assured me that the house on which she had the listing was the one next to it which was exactly what I was hoping. I needed no more than a couple of seconds before I said "I don't think that little house is for sale." "What are you talking about?" she replied, "I know the owner personally and I have the listing and I know that it is for sale. I also know the people who own the large house and they know the little house is for sale!" She seemed to be getting quite upset with me so I thought I had better calm things down a little. "I'm sorry," I apologized, "I wasn't saying that I didn't believe you, it's just that I know something you don't." "Oh, really," she replied, "And what would that be?" "That little house is not for sale because it has already been sold!" At that stage I thought she was going to really get upset when I saw that she was staring at me, stuttering a little, "Bbbbb.bbbbb." "Now hold on a minute," I said, "It's not for sale because that is my house, or it will be, just as soon as you get all the paperwork done". There was a short silence while she took a couple of deep breaths. And then came the questions! "How can you say that? You haven't even been inside it, you haven't seen the front, you don't even know how many bed-rooms it has, how do you know your wife will like it, when is she coming from N.Carolina to see it?" and on and on until she was getting short of breath again. Finally she calmed down and I told her that all her concerns were valid but they would all be taken care of, one way or another. I just knew that this was going to be my house. From the very first sight I had of that pretty little lake-side shack, as I called it, with just a concrete block sea-wall separating it from the water, I knew I had found my little piece of paradise here on Swan Lake. I sincerely believe that my Creator intended for me to be here and I'm pretty sure the local wild-life are grateful for that too. About fifty Mallards took off when I opened the sun-room door this morning and when I came back inside so as not to disturb them from their breakfast, one of the Muscovy ducks settled on the top of the handrail so he could look inside to see if I was O.K. Who could ask for anything more?

A MOVING FOOTBALL HELMET

A few days ago I was taking the "Kids," Sammy and Dee for their early morning drive and I guess we were all in a bit of a fog; even Sammy didn't bark, which was very unusual for him. A hundred yards or so in front of us there appeared to be a junior sized, black, football helmet rolling across the road in our lane. "What on Earth is that?" I asked myself and, having checked the mirror to see if anyone was following, I started to brake. We approached the object and then stopped about two yards short of it. By then another car had caught up with us and when I stopped, the driver had to give us a blast on his horn. I stepped out of the car and, not wishing to start a commotion that early in the morning, I threw him a hand-wave, using all my fingers, and bent down to examine the strangest looking turtle I had ever seen. It was flat on the bottom but the rest of the shell was almost a complete globe. All the other turtles I've seen around here have been relatively thin compared to this one, except for the Snapping turtle variety which looks like a heavy, knobbly suit of armor. Well, whatever his lineage, the occupant of the shell seemed to be anxious to get going so I carefully deposited him in the grass verge, the way he had been heading. The driver that I had held up pulled around me and, with a brief tire squeal and a blast on his horn raced up the road. I gave him a farewell wave, again with a handful of fingers. You see, I still have traces of being an English gentleman in spite of my growing redneckedness!

It was only the next day when I encountered the exact opposite of the Football helmet turtle. Fortunately I was driving slowly; the speed limit around Swan Lake is only 25 mph; and I was able to stop in plenty of time to avoid running over a tiny little turtle who was doing his best to hurry across the road towards the lake. His shell was shaped like an elongated circle and only about half an inch thick in the center. The edges were almost paper thin and the whole thing looked somewhat fragile. Anyway, with no-one behind me, I took the time to gently pick him up and place him in the grass on the lake edge, admonishing him to look both ways before attempting to cross the road again.

I have seen and handled many different shapes and sizes of turtle shells in the twenty years that I have lived here but the latest two were totally different from any of the previous shells, or carapaces as they are called, and I started thinking about what happens when a turtle outgrows his shell and needs a bigger "house?" When his shell becomes too tight when he grows, does he just crawl out of it and get into a bigger one and, if so, where does the bigger shell come from? Does each pond, lake, swamp, stream, and river have hidden stock-rooms, deep in the muddy banks somewhere, where discarded shells are stored for later use by the youngsters, growing up? And, if so, who collects them and stores them away for a time when a needy turtle is looking for one? There should be thousands of empty shells laying around unless there is an army of collectors, working the waterways.

O.K. I'm sorry. I got carried away with my thoughts back there. That's what I get for reading too many of Peggy Renfroe's stories. That lady has an incredible imagination and her books are a whole lot of fun to read. Try one, I know you'll love it, regardless of your age.

Well, my time is up for now. I'll be getting back with you soon with some more tales of my feathered and furry friends on Swan Lake, so, for now, I'll just say "

'Bye y'all,"

A SUMMER UNIFORM

Outside my window hangs a large red container of Humming Bird food, now only about one third full. The birds seem to have taken a rest for now and I don't blame them when the temperature is in the high nineties. The heat doesn't seem to bother their antagonists, in their yellow and black striped jackets who take advantage of the birds' absence by sucking up as much of the juice as possible while they have a clear field. I just saw my favorite H.B. who I call "Redneck", make an exploratory visit to the feeder but he hurriedly called off his mission when a fat yellow jacket tried to ambush him from his hide-out under the feeder. You know, every Summer for about the last five years there has always been one H.B. with a red collar visiting the feeder. I've never seen more than one at a time. Could it possibly be the same bird? Most of the "Feeder fights" take place in the evenings and continue almost until the light dies. I don't pull the blind down after sunset and I can sit and watch the activity in silhouette.

One interesting variation that I've noted a few times lately has been a small H.B. has settled down over the feeder stations and turned his head sideways as though taking a nap. It only takes a few seconds for a much larger bird to hover over him while she prods him with her needle-nose to wake him up. I know I'm making some suppositions there, but as Si would say, "Hey! I'm not lof lightning. I couldn't help thinking of those AFV clips not lein' Jack" On one occasion, Junior refused to move and I thought he might be in trouble. I carefully opened the window and reached for him to see if I could help him. He woke up in a hurry then and took off like a flash of lightning. I couldn't help thinking of those AFV clips which have shown small children, in high chairs, sleeping with their heads in their food. Maybe we're not so different after all. But it sure would be fun to be able to fly like that.

Talking of yellow-jackets on the bird-feeder brings thoughts of the fig-tree which now covers a large part of the back yard, extending over the lean-to shed within four feet, or so, of the feeder. I missed out on pruning the tree during the early Spring, for one reason or another, and now I am faced with a huge, bushy tree, laden with firm, fat, fruit. And all within easy reach of a yellow-jacket hangout whose occupants also enjoy the little delicacies. And I love figs! I'm looking forward to the fruit when it ripens, if not the fight which I'm going to have to get them! Now would be a good time to buy shares in the Company which manufactures "Deep Woods Off." I'm probably going to be bathing in the stuff! But all is not entirely lost, I have another, smaller fig tree in the front of the house which is also doing well, "fruit-wise", in spite of being frost-bitten during that crazy off and on again early Spring that we suffered this year. It looks a little odd being so bushy, with black spikes sticking up above the bush for several feet. I know, I should have pruned them off several months ago but for one reason or another, well, you know how that goes by now!

Well, the temperature on my outside thermometer reads 99.4F and even the yellow jackets are taking a break. "Redneck" just called in for a couple of seconds and stared at me through the window. I'm sure he was asking me to get a refill in the feeder ready for this evening's entertainment. I'd better get on with my "butlering" duties and I'm sure my Muscovy friends would appreciate some dinner. An appetite seems to be the one thing they're never short of. Just remember the motto of "Duck Depot" - Dogs and Ducks Rule!

Others books by Don Sweetenham

Bumps in the Road

Bumps in the Road 2

Reflections on Swan Lake